The Politics of Regulation

Also by Alison Young

THE FIXERS: Crisis Management in British Politics (*with Trevor Smith*)

The Politics of Regulation

Privatized Utilities in Britain

Alison Young
Research Fellow
Centre for Management under Regulation
Warwick Business School
Warwick University

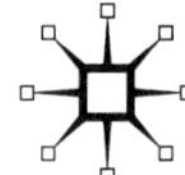

First published 2001 by
PALGRAVE
Houndmills, Basingstoke, Hampshire RG21 6XS and
175 Fifth Avenue, New York, N.Y. 10010
Companies and representatives throughout the world

PALGRAVE is the new global academic imprint of
St. Martin's Press LLC Scholarly and Reference Division and
Palgrave Publishers Ltd (formerly Macmillan Press Ltd).

ISBN 0–333–92750–8

This book is printed on paper suitable for recycling and made from fully managed and sustained forest sources.

A catalogue record for this book is available from the British Library.

Library of Congress Cataloging-in-Publication Data
Young, Alison.
　　The politics of regulation : privatized utilities in Britain / Alison Young.
　　　　p. cm.
　　Includes bibliographical references and index.
　　ISBN 0–333–92750–8
　　1. Public utilities—Deregulation—Great Britain.
　　2. Privatization—Great Britain. I. Title.
　　HD2768.G74 Y68 2001
　　363.6'0941—dc21

00–053045

10　9　8　7　6　5　4　3　2　1
10　09　08　07　06　05　04　03　02　01

Printed and bound in Great Britain by
Antony Rowe Ltd, Chippenham, Wiltshire

For my mother

Contents

Preface

The privatization of utilities was a major innovation in British politics and both the principles and the implementation have been the subject of vigorous debate since 1984 when BT became the first state-owned utility to be sold off. The passing of a new Utilities Act in 2000 marked the end of a preliminary phase that has witnessed much public criticism but ultimately seen a measure of acceptance.

This book attempts to analyze the rationale for returning the nationalized industries to private ownership, the activities of the regulators who were appointed to oversee them and the mechanisms put in place to ensure accountability. The emphasis is on the politics of regulation and a narrative is presented of the main events that illuminate this process over the period since privatization. Greater stress on consumer issues developed gradually, but there were several episodes in which consumers were dramatically failed by the privatized companies. The MMC, now the Competition Commission, played an important role in establishing the RPI−X formula, introducing competition and the establishing the accounting disciplines which underlay economic regulation. Parliamentary select committees tried, though without notable success, to improve accountability. The problems of integrating environmental policy came increasingly to the fore. Some areas receive briefer treatment – telecoms for instance, where both the regulator and the industry have for several years asserted that their business was not a utility. The rail industry, presenting a very different range of problems, is excluded altogether. Similarly, no coverage is given of the European input to regulation or the influence of financial institutions. Though the emphasis is on politics, those who seek a more economics-based approach will find plenty of sources in the references.

I have been fortunate over the last three years to be a Research Fellow at the Centre for Management under Regulation at Warwick Business School. During the writing of this book the encouragement and support of the centre's Director, Professor Catherine Waddams, has been invaluable. I would also like to thank all my colleagues at the centre, especially Lin Fitzgerald, Catherine Mitchell and Diane Sharratt, for their advice and help.

I would also like to thank Morten Hviid, Patrick Law, Michael Doble, Graham McKie and Alex Young all of whom commented on various chapters. I am grateful to all of them, but especially to my husband, Charles Young, for his help and forbearance over so many months.

List of Abbreviations

ABC	Activity Based Costing
BAA	British Airports Authority
BATNEEC	Best Available Technology Not Entailing Excessive Cost
BGT	British Gas Trading
BPEO	Best Practicable Environmental Option
BT	British Telecom
CA	Consumers Association
CCGT	Combined Cycle Gas Turbine
CHP	Combined Heat and Power
CLA	Country Landowners Association
CRI	Centre for the Study of Regulated Industries
CSC	Customer Service Committee
DGFT	Director General of Fair Trading
DoI	Department of Industry
DTI	Department of Trade and Industry
ECC	Electricity Consumers Council
ECCCG	Electricity Consumers Councils Chairmens' Group
EESoPS	Energy Efficiency Standards of Performance
ERM	Exchange Rate Mechanism
ESI	Electricity Supply Industry
EST	Energy Saving Trust
EU	European Union
FFL	Fossil Fuel Levy
FGD	Flue Gas Desulphurisation
FMI	Financial Management Initiative
GECC	Gas and Electricity Consumers Council
GW	Gigawatt
HEES	Home Energy Efficiency Scheme
IEA	Institute of Economic Affairs
IPPR	Institute for Public Policy Research
kW	kilowatt
LBS	London Business School
MMC	Monopolies and Mergers Commission (now Competition Commission)
MW	Megawatt
NAO	National Audit Office

NCC	National Consumer Council
NECC	National Electricity Consumers Council
NEDO	National Economic Development Office
NETA	New Electricity Trading Arrangements
NFU	National Farmers Union
NFFO	Non Fossil Fuel Obligation
NIE	Northern Ireland Electricity
OFFER	Office of Electricity Regulation
Ofgas	Office of Gas Supply
Ofgem	Office of Gas and Electricity Markets
OFT	Office of Fair Trading
OFTEL	Office of Telecommunications
Ofwat	Office of Water Services
ONCC	Ofwat National Consumer Council
PAC	Public Accounts Committee
PES	Public Electricity Supplier
PUAF	Public Utilities Access Forum
REC	Regional Electricity Company
SWALEC	South Wales Electricity
SWEB	South Western Electricity Board
SWW	South West Water
TIC	Trade and Industry Committee
TXU	Texas Utilities
WASC	Water and Sewerage Company
WOC	Water Only Company

1
From Nationalization to Privatization

'The largest transfer of property since the dissolution of the monasteries.'*

Caustically described by Harold Macmillan as 'selling the family silver', and by Tony Benn as the plunder of state assets, the privatization programme of the Thatcher government was one of the most radical policy changes in twentieth century British politics. The nationalized industries were the legacy of the post-war Labour government and, the steel industry apart, it was one which had been accepted by subsequent Conservative administrations. Indeed the Heath government of 1970–4 had greatly increased public ownership. This consensus was never complete, some in the Conservative party had always nurtured a dislike of state-owned enterprises and as their performance deteriorated in the late 1970s this view was more widely held. Norman Tebbit summed it up thus: 'The nationalized industries have been letting us down for years' (Newman, 1986, p. 7).

The privatization of the telecoms, gas, water and electricity industries from 1984 to 1991 represented a major realignment of the boundaries between the state and private sectors of the UK. At the same time as they were sold on the stock exchange, in flotations of a size previously unimaginable, a regulator for each of these 'utilities' was appointed. These people, originally four in number, now three since gas and electricity regulation have been unified, possess huge influence over a large sector of British industry and exercise what some see as excessive discretion over prices and competition in these fundamental undertakings.

*Quoted in Veljanovski, 1987, p. 1.

Since privatization, the industries concerned and their regulators have been the focus of intense media and public attention and occasional virulent criticism. Consumers found it hard to think of these companies as private profit-making businesses; shareholders often felt their interests were being ignored. Since those early days, apart from a few headline-catching episodes, the public and the city have become accustomed to the new regime and consumers have received greater benefits than at the start. But it is still not possible to keep regulation out of politics, which was one of the aims of privatization.

Writing on this subject has however, to a large extent been dominated by economists. Most of the published literature, in journals and from organizations such as the Institute of Economic Affairs (IEA) and the Centre for the study of Regulated Industries (CRI) concentrates almost exclusively on the economics of regulation. In the press, too, unless there is a headline catching story such as the one in the summer of 1996 about Yorkshire Water trucking water supplies long distances, coverage is confined to the business pages. But this is a field which is irrevocably political, and in which economic theory, at least at the outset, was not much of a guide to action on encouraging competition. Though many of the motivations or justifications behind the privatization programme were political, and they also included the government's need for the proceeds of the flotations, much of the advice sought and given has been from economists. The very structure of the industries is the result of political pressure from one interest or another. For instance the gas industry was sold off as a single huge corporation largely because of the powerful influence of Sir Denis Rooke, chairman of what was then the British Gas Corporation. The electricity supply industry was divided up in a rather uneven manner, with National Power having 70 per cent of the market and PowerGen only 30 per cent, because of the problem of the nuclear sector, of which Mrs Thatcher was an enthusiastic champion. When it was finally conceded that a successful sell-off would be jeopardized if the nuclear stations were included in the deal, the respective shares of the two other generating companies were altered to 50 per cent and 32 per cent respectively. Approximately 14 per cent went to Nuclear Electric which remained at that time in the public sector. Cento Veljanovski of the IEA commented, only half-joking, that the electricity industry might have been better off if it had been given the structure of the gas industry and vice versa!

If the privatization process was one of political compromise and dealing, often behind closed doors, the period of regulation which succeeded it was also highly political. As one American economist,

Irving Stelzer declared: 'Regulation is a business in which people make a difference' (Stelzer, 1988, p. 78). The following pages will attempt to demonstrate the truth of this remark. An attempt will also be made to throw light on the problems of accountability thrown up by the regulatory system and to assess how successful the regulators have been.

Privatization became a main theme of the Conservative governments of the 1980s as the result of a variety of ideas and pressures. The most clearly articulated at the outset was the strand of ideology which wanted to 'roll back the frontiers of the state' and get the government 'off the people's backs', what Vincent Wright called a 'paradigm shift away from dirigisme' (Wright, 1995). This constituted a clear rejection of the consensus politics that had held sway for most of the post war years. The impulse to privatize was accompanied by a drive towards greater efficiency and the introduction of private business methods into government. Though strongly associated with the Conservative government and especially perhaps with Margaret Thatcher, it was also part and parcel of a much broader change in views on public administration and government expenditure throughout the Western world in the mid- to late-1970s. The sharp increases in oil prices were an important influence, in particular in the UK after the Callaghan government was forced to seek a loan from the IMF in 1976. Reductions in public expenditure and the defeat of inflation became the top priorities.

Managerialism, or what became known as the New Public Management, also had a part to play. This new approach, associated by many with the rise of the New Right, especially in Australia and New Zealand emphasised the three Es: Economy, Efficiency and Effectiveness. It stressed management not policy, and focused on performance appraisal and efficiency, targets, cost cutting, contracting out and disaggregation of public bureaucracies. This was first applied in the early days of the Thatcher government to the Whitehall bureaucracy. One of Mrs Thatcher's first actions on becoming Prime Minister was to appoint Derek Rayner, the managing director of Marks and Spencer, to head her efficiency unit; he instituted the so-called 'Rayner scrutinies' which eventually culminated in the Next Steps agencies, by means of which many functions previously subject to close supervision by central government were removed from Whitehall. This gave rise to problems about accountability and where the line should be drawn between policy and operations. A striking example of this was the dispute between the Director of the Prison Service, Derek Lewis, and the Home Secretary, Michael Howard, in 1995. Similar questions about accountability arose for the regulators.

The privatization programme was part of a wave of deregulation which included council house sales, compulsory competitive tendering and the sale of enterprises which had become part of the public sector as part of a rescue operation, such as British Shipbuilders and the National Freight Corporation, acquired over the years by governments of both persuasions. The Conservative government's view that the private sector was inherently more efficient was shared by some of the public, and these sales attracted interest but not a great deal of controversy. Though the prime motive for the sales was the reduction of the PSBR, there was also an ideological underpinning. Private sector management, the argument went, is bound to be more efficient than that in the public sector because it is not cushioned by the state's obligation to cover its losses, what economists would call competition in the capital market. On the contrary, the threat of bankruptcy or takeover provided by market forces – even if somewhat restricted – compels companies to run more efficiently. Shareholders reinforce this pressure. But many would not accept the assumption that ownership makes the crucial difference; competition is also necessary for the market to work properly.

The utilities

The state-owned companies in the first wave of privatization for the most part operated in markets in which private companies were already competing; for instance British Aerospace (February 1981), Cable and Wireless (October 1981), Britoil (November 1982) and the British Steel Corporation (December 1988), Amersham International (February 1982), National Freight Corporation, Associated British Ports (February 1983). Privatizing the utilities was another matter. These industries have a number of distinctive characteristics that made selling them off problematic, with the consequence that political involvement was greater. The first is that their products are not commodities like any other, they are basic necessities, essential to life. Water and fuel are as necessary as food and shelter. Telecommunications may be an exception to this, though access to a telephone can be argued to be a necessary condition of social inclusion. The relative inelasticity of demand for fuel and water and even telephone services is an indicator of this (see for example Armstrong, Cowan and Vickers, 1994, p. 209). Though gas and electricity are to a certain extent substitutes for each other, there is none for water. Since they are basic requirements, security of supply has been considered important especially at times of peak demands, and obligations have traditionally been imposed on utilities to supply all consumers who want them, including the poor and those who live in remote places.

As well as being necessities gas, electricity and water, and even telecoms, though to a lesser extent nowadays, are network industries. This is obvious enough, but its importance lies in the fact that the need for a network is a barrier to entry, making the cost of entry to an industry prohibitively expensive, and inefficient in the sense that it is cheaper to have a single provider – in other words a natural monopoly. The combination of an essential good and monopoly power resulted in regulation to protect the consumer long before the Nationalization Acts of the Attlee government, which simplified numerous complex regulations and established them firmly as public services owned by the nation (though the water industry was not effectively nationalized until the 1970s and there have always been small private companies supplying water and a private telephone company in Hull). In addition the supply of all of these goods is as essential to the whole economy as to individuals; they are part of the infrastructure of the nation which permits the rest of industry, whether manufacturing or service, to function. A further distinctive characteristic is that they give rise to externalities – spin-off effects that can have an impact upon society at large and on individuals not directly involved. There is a social cost incurred over and above the cost of supplying the service. The most obvious example of this is pollution; externalities provide another reason why this kind of industry is virtually always subject to regulation, environmental perhaps as well as economic.

For all of these reasons, from 1945 to the 1980s the industries remained nationalized and to a large extent out of the public eye. Since privatization they have been under the spotlight. The sales of assets raised nearly £70 billion and some of the flotations were the biggest in post-war European history, several topping £5 billion. As a result, 'Regulation is the new border between the state and industry. It is also the battleground for ideas on industrial policy and how the economy should be run' (Veljanovski, 1991, p. 4). But what was expected to be a move to greater freedom, has in fact resulted in far more regulation than had been expected. The light touch that had been hoped for has turned out to be an unexpectedly heavy hand, and the regulators themselves have also been the subject of fierce criticism.

The experience of nationalization

Both supporters and critics of privatization take the view that it was a policy the Conservative government adopted with little premeditation.

Similarly, it cannot be claimed that the Nationalization Acts of the 1940s which brought into existence the giant public sector industries which were to be for so long a feature of the political/economic landscape were the result of long and careful preparation. Though the document *Labour and the New Social Order*, published in 1918, demanded immediate nationalization of the coal mines, electricity and railways, what little preparatory work had been done was very theoretical, placing great emphasis on 'independent and disinterested experts' (Kelf-Cohen, 1969, p. 25). So, when Emmanuel Shinwell became Minister of Fuel and Power in 1945 there was no blueprint in Labour party files to help him to put the policy into effect, merely resolutions passed at Labour party conferences.

The party was committed to planning 'from the ground up' and to redistribution of wealth but its purpose was also to rescue these basic industries from over-complex regulation that had grown up over the previous half century. The telephone company had been nationalized in 1912 after thirty years of disorganization. The creation of the Central Electricity Board during the Baldwin government had brought order to the chaos of municipal power stations. There was substantial cross-party support for the state ownership of electricity, gas, railways and coal. Indeed, it was surprising that the electricity industry had not been nationalized earlier. One-third of the gas industry had been municipalized, the other two-thirds consisted of 700 private companies, and a committee that reported in December 1945 had recommended its nationalization. The railways had effectively been brought under state control in the war years. The success of the mobilisation of the economy for the war effort had a big influence on what was done after the war ended. Various other public corporations had come into being including the BBC (1926) and the London Passenger Transport Board (LPTB) that had been set up in 1933. As Minister of Transport in the second Ramsay MacDonald government, Herbert Morrison had devised the LPTB, which he described as 'a combination of public ownership, public accountability and business management for public ends' (quoted in Hennessy, 1994, p. 197). It was the LPTB in particular, which provided the model for the post-war nationalized industries – what came to be known as the Morrisonian corporation.

Reflecting the strong Labour belief in the economies of scale and the value of central planning, the coal and railway industries were established on the same monopoly model as gas and electricity. So, as with the privatization programme forty years later, economic and political motives were mixed, but the change of ownership was assumed by those carrying it out to be the solution to most of the problems. The nationalization acts were intended to improve the efficiency of the capitalist economy; by the time Labour gained power in 1945, there was never any question of workers' control. It was recognised that regulation of these industries would be necessary, as it had been in the past, and that their activities and development would need to form part of the promised economic planning. But how this would be linked with their ordinary operations remained unclear. Morrison assumed a slight and occasional influence by government on the industries. He also naively thought that once nationalized, they would be run efficiently, with improving quality and falling prices. They were supposed to combine commercial flexibility with political accountability, and were theoretically autonomous. Chairmen and boards were appointed by the minister of the sponsoring department, who was able to issue general directions to the board and had to give approval for substantial capital investment. He also presented the annual report to parliament. In practice, the arm's length control originally foreseen by Morrison did not take place. One reason for this was that the aims and purposes of the industries were not clearly set down. One aim was to provide a cheap and reliable service to all, another to operate efficiently. It was intended that they should break even, 'taking one year with another' that is, tread a path between making monopoly profits and running deficits, so pricing was clearly of great importance.

But ministers could not resist the temptation to interfere. The division between operational and policy matters was often difficult to define. Although the power to direct boards was never used, at least in the early years, an immense amount of informal pressure was applied – known as the 'lunchtime directive' – and ministers constantly interfered in pricing. Though there was a serious fuel shortage in the 1940s, prices were not raised; and in the 1970s and 1980s, under both Labour and Conservative governments, prices were altered up or down for reasons of macro-economic policy. Investment decisions had to be approved annually by the Treasury, with civil servants second-guessing what was being decided in the corporations. Political capture, as it would be called nowadays, was complete.

The House of Commons was also keen to become involved. The Select Committee on Nationalized Industries, which faced considerable ministerial opposition to its activities, when it was set up in 1955, eventually got going with a proper enquiry in 1956, but found in Kelf-Cohen's words, that 'parliamentary accountability was a will o'the wisp' (Kelf-Cohen, 1969, p. 177). The legislation did not provide a real role for parliament to play. None the less the committee did have some influence. The chairman of the Coal Board told the committee '...we are not flesh, fish or good red herring. We are not a commercial undertaking; we are not a public service; we are a bit of each' (Kelf-Cohen, 1969, p. 166).

During the 1950s the industries more or less broke even, and prices were held fairly steady, though little attempt was made to develop guidance on investment, pricing and related matters. But as time went on the confusion over the appropriate extent of ministerial control and about how responsibilities should be divided led to continuing problems, especially with those industries that were in decline, such as the railways and coal. Faced with serious economic problems and a threat to sterling, the government published a White Paper in 1961 that set financial targets for the first time and implicitly established a pricing policy. In 1967 these were tightened up and detailed pricing and investment policies were introduced, as well as modern analytical tools such as discounted cash flows and cost benefit analysis, which were not always consistent with each other. Pricing was to be based on long-run marginal cost; the government would be consulted on major price rises and could refer them to the Prices and Incomes Board. Attempts in the 1970s to reaffirm targets and reduce ministerial interference did not provide the vital ingredient – the making of policy. The Callaghan government of 1976–9 rejected NEDO's suggestion of policy boards that might have provided a coherent link between government policy and what was done in the industries. By 1978, ministers' powers of intervention had been strengthened still further, financial targets had become the primary instrument of control, new external financing limits had been introduced and prices had to be set at a level which would meet the target.

The Thatcher years

By the time of the Conservative election victory in 1979, the economic climate indicated that a more drastic approach to the nationalized industries was required. The intellectual climate was also changing. The static world optimistically envisaged by Morrison in which everyone would do their best was being replaced by a more cynical approach in the shape of Public Choice Theory or the 'economics of politics'. This concept, which originated at the University of Virginia, recognized the importance of information and of incentives and used game theory, seeing individuals as motivated by narrow egotistic concerns.

On this view, publicly provided services deprived the consumer of choice; privatization was therefore desirable with or without competition.

By extension it discredited the 'Woodrow Wilson view of bureaucracy: choose a few good men and give them the power to follow the public interest' (Bosanquet, 1981, p. 339). Even the existence of externalities did not provide a clear case for public intervention.

In spite of the problems associated with the nationalized industries, selling them off had not been seriously considered by the mainstream of the Conservative party prior to the Conservative election victory in 1979; only the National Freight Corporation featured in the manifesto. The wilder right wing fringes certainly had looked at it – 'denationalization' was the term in those days. In common with so many other measures of reform that Margaret Thatcher was to turn into political reality, some consideration had been given to the idea both before and during the Heath government. The idea probably first came into public view in a book by the management guru Peter Drucker, *The Age of Discontinuity*, published in 1969. During the mid-1960s, when the Conservative party under Heath was in opposition, Nicholas Ridley, a confirmed right winger, 'a Thatcherite before Thatcher' (Ranelagh, 1992, p. 12), had proposed a radical programme of denationalization while he was chairman of the national industry policy committee. Heath suppressed this as being quite unrealistic and politically suicidal. His biographer comments that at this stage it was a 'crackpot fantasy of the far right' (Campbell, 1993, p. 235). All the same, when Heath became prime minister after the 1970 general election, there were renewed calls for denationalization and according to Anthony Sampson, chronicler of the nation's political anatomy, Heath initially encouraged Ridley, now at the Department of Industry and those who shared his views. However, when Heath's non-interventionist policy underwent a major U-turn, Ridley resigned and Heath left government with a bigger public sector than when he had arrived.

By the end of the decade, Ridley was still strongly opposed to the nationalized industries; and according to his own memoirs, he dusted down the old report of ten years earlier for Sir Keith Joseph, newly appointed Secretary of State for Industry in the Thatcher government. 'It was almost identical…suitably updated' (Ridley, 1991, p. 15). Much of the report focused on tighter financial discipline, but the utilities were well down the list of priorities for privatization. As Sir Ian Gilmour commented 'even the most ideological Thatcherites had not advocated denationalizing the natural monopolies' (Gilmour, 1993, p. 120).

Sir Keith, Mrs Thatcher's inspiration, had issued a reading list to his advisers and civil servants. This, described as a 'useful summary of the New Right' included Adam Smith's *Wealth of Nations* (1776),

Schumpeter's *Capitalism, Socialism and Democracy* (1943) and *The Fallacy of the Mixed Economy* (1978) by Stephen Littlechild. Depoliticization is a theme that runs through the list. David Young, later Lord Young of Graffham, was among those who were issued with a copy; he had been appointed an industrial adviser immediately after the election and at the end of 1980 he was given responsibility for privatization. He took a particular interest in British Telecom (BT) and the Post Office and later became Secretary of State for Trade and Industry and later still chairman of Cable and Wireless. He was of the opinion that BT should be broken up into regional companies on the pattern of the Baby Bells in the USA.

Another future cabinet minister who was concerned about the nationalized industries was a young fellow of All Souls, John Redwood. In 1980 he published a book with the title *Public Enterprise in Crisis*; he favoured liberalization of the telecommunications legislation and various other competitive measures, but not actually selling off the utilities. Indeed at this time, though he saw that power generation, unlike the National Grid, is not a natural monopoly, he did not suggest breaking up the Central Electricity Generating Board (CEGB).

Sir Christopher Foster, economist, arch privatizer and author of a book on the subject, quotes Oliver Letwin as saying 'We had no coherent policy … it came upon us gradually and by accident and by a leap of faith' (Foster, 1992, p. 109). Certainly as time went on, faith seemed to be an important factor. One of the chief evangelists was John Moore, a junior minister at the Treasury, whose responsibilities included privatization and the Inland Revenue. He made a series of speeches from the end of 1983 on the importance of privatization, which gave the programme a coherence it had previously lacked. Over the next few years, the justifications and rationale for the policy were gradually produced and polished. Privatization was not a key issue in the 1983 election, just as it had not been in 1979. But by this time BT was well on the way to the private sector; later Moore declared: 'where competition is impractical, privatization policies have now been developed to such an extent that regulated private ownership of natural monopolies is preferable to nationalization' (Foster, 1992, p. 124).

In the meantime, attempts were still being made to regain some sort of control over those industries. Disputes and disagreements between government departments and nationalized industries led to two separate approaches. The first was to try and improve relations. But Mrs Thatcher did not like Sir Derek Ezra or Sir Peter Parker and personal relations were always crucial to disputes during her premiership.

The 1980 Competition Act extended the terms of reference of the MMC to include the operations of the nationalized industries. The Central Policy Review Staff, better known as the 'think tank', was also asked to look at the problem. It recommended more clearly defined objectives and the establishment of business groups. A leaked copy was strongly criticized by *The Economist* and Thatcher and Lawson found their suggestions equally unappealing, so much so that the think tank was abolished immediately after the 1983 election.

The External Financing Limits (EFLs) of those nationalized industries which were accumulating losses became a serious problem and for those which were not, pressure was put on them to contribute more to reducing the PSBR. There was direct intervention in domestic gas prices. The Treasury was forcing negative EFLs on the electricity industry, the post office and the airlines. According to one analysis, the nationalized industries were costing each taxpayer £300 a year (Jenkins, 1996, p. 27). The PSBR, this 'dubious and manipulable statistic' (Heald, 1988, p. 34), was the lodestar of economic policy in the late 1970s after the IMF intervention and through at least the early 1980s. When public enterprises were sold their capital investment programmes were removed from the public sector accounts. In addition, what was raised from the sales of assets was deducted from public expenditure totals. This quirky approach – 'statistical cosmetics' (Rees, 1986, p. 23) – resulted in large falls in the PSBR total. The flow of funds provided by sales of assets were very attractive to a government which was having to hold down public expenditure and wanted to cut taxes (Rees, 1986, p. 21). But it may be the case that the EFLs were after 1981 used to encourage those in the management of the industries in the direction of privatization (Heald, 1988, p. 34).

Apart from the desire of the Treasury to relieve pressure on the financial situation, there was naturally a series of motives connected with the recent dismal history of the nationalized industries. Transfer to the private sector would, it was argued, encourage innovation and competition, and would also reduce the power of the public sector unions. Strikes had had a debilitating effect on the economy during the 1970s and early 1980s. In addition, widening share ownership by selling shares to ordinary people, including workers in those industries, would further undermine union power by giving the people a stake in popular capitalism. Thus rolling back the state would simultaneously increase efficiency and depoliticize the relations between the government and the industries. Central government departments seemed to have a deep ignorance about enterprise – which had been the main reason for Morrison's 'arm's length' proposals in the 1940s. A considerable influence on the privatization programme was the theory of contestable markets developed in the United States when airlines were being deregulated.

The single most important factor in sparking the privatization programme however, was the financing of investment for these industries. They wanted to be free to borrow on the capital markets. Publicly owned industries were not permitted to do this, because it was seen as virtually identical to government borrowing but also competed with the private sector. The effects of this restriction first became clear in the case of BT. The telephone service was at that time very poor, with long waiting times and rising complaints. By the time the idea of floating BT on the stock market began to take shape, selling off public sector assets had become almost commonplace. BT was different though, because of its size and because it was a public service and because it became the pattern for other privatizations which were to follow.

Privatization was to be a unifying theme for a divided Conservative party, which could not agree on macro economic policy. Its success, politically at least was partly due to equally deep divisions in the opposition and possibly also to the longest bull market seen in the post war period. Though influenced by American regulation, it was claimed (by Nigel Lawson) as a genuine new idea (Lawson, 1992, p. 198). As has already been mentioned, the idea of privatization was part of a general shift in views on government and administration. This new intellectual climate was fostered in the think tanks and research foundations that nourished the thinking of the Conservative party. But though the desire to transfer publicly owned enterprises into the private sector gained greater acceptance as time passed, there were no detailed plans on how this should be put into practice.

The first utility privatization – BT

Moves to improve and liberalize the telephone service had begun in 1980. The British Telecommunications Act of 1981 split BT from the post office and ended its de facto monopoly. Sir Keith Joseph, Secretary of State for Industry (May 1979 to September 1981) asked Professor Michael Beesley, who was, like Littlechild, from Birmingham University – and indeed a close friend and colleague of his – to write a report on how this might be done. The question at issue was whether value added services (VANS) should be permitted to be provided by firms other than BT. Beesley recommended in effect that other firms should be allowed to enter the market, but the government preferred to give permission to the Mercury Project that was to build an optical fibre network. BT itself was in great need of a major investment programme. Here the problem of nationalized industries' capital expenditure reached a crunch point. The attempt to finance investment by issuing 'Buzby Bonds' came to nothing largely because of the legal problems of distinguishing them from public sector borrowing. A price rise which would have enabled the investment to be largely self-financing had to be humiliatingly reversed when the targets for investment were not met. Privatization was hit upon as a means of reconciling the investment programme with the government's strict limits on borrowing. Patrick Jenkin, who had succeeded Keith Joseph, made the announcement in July 1982.

In establishing a new system for regulating the utilities, the government wanted to avoid some of the pitfalls of the past but also drew a good deal on American experience. Rate of return regulation, as widely used in the USA, seemed to British eyes to have resulted in a system that too easily became bogged down in long drawn out and expensive legalistic hearings and appeared to lack efficiency incentives.

Involved in the consideration of how profits or prices were to be controlled was a working party at the Department of Industry (DoI) together with David Wolfson, head of the policy unit at No. 10 and an old friend and former business colleague of David Young, a fixer and close to the prime minister. The matter was receiving attention at the highest level. Like Littlechild and Beesley, Young was an IEA supporter. US experience suggested to them that a maximum rate of return might do, but Alan Walters, the Prime Minister's adviser on economic matters, strongly opposed this method, because it was tantamount to a marginal tax rate of 100 per cent which smacked far too much of socialism. Walters' preferred method was a profit levy which would be inversely related to output – in other words the greater the expansion the lower the rate at which the levy would be charged.

This was when Stephen Littlechild came onto the scene. He was to become perhaps the single most influential person in the saga of privatizing and regulating Britain's utility industries and certainly the most controversial. Not only did he write the first report on how BT should be regulated, which contained the price cap formula RPI − X, but he was also later responsible for the White Paper on the regulation of the water companies, advised on the privatization of the ESI and then became the first electricity regulator. So the gas industry – and the BAA – were the only ones with which he did not have a close connection, though they too were subject to the RPI−X price cap regime.

Patrick Jenkin, expressing a preference for 'regulation with a light rein', presented these ideas to Littlechild on 28 October 1982 for him to consider and report back. He and Beesley were the only two prominent economists in the country who had worked on the economics of telecommunications. The articles they wrote together (Beesley and Littlechild, 1983 and 1989) were major contributions to the literature on regulation. With help from the DoI, the Treasury, the PM's office, Kleinwort Benson and Warburgs, Littlechild produced a report in six weeks. Littlechild was aware that US views on rate of return regulation had been changing, and was dubious about Walters' scheme which would not foster competition and would also have required the introduction of a new tax. He therefore decided that a successful regulatory mechanism would have to be a precision instrument, since local calls were the main concern. Three strands of thought came together. A member of the Warburg team thought that an element of the ill-fated Buzby Bond might be useful: this related price cuts to performance. The Monopolies and Mergers Commission (MMC) in a separate case had introduced a maximum price rise per year related to index of costs on the products of the London Rubber Company. American regulation had introduced automatic 'escalator clauses'. A combination of these two approaches would incorporate stronger incentives and greater flexibility than a rate of return mechanism.

Thus RPI−X was born. Prices would be capped to a level below the rate of inflation for a period of years. The report also included the suggestion that quality standards should be required; and quality did later become a problem. It is a common experience that having fixed X the regulator finds it necessary to control some other aspects because of unintended consequences. Price cap regulation has been described as a classic case in which practice is far out ahead of theory – a true policy innovation (Brauetigam and Panzar, 1993, p. 197).

Though the formula has mainly been a success, in that consumers have benefited from lower prices apart from in the water industry, and political interference has been at a much lower level than in the 1970s and 1980s, in the early years, low levels of X led to embarrassingly high profits (Foster, 1992, p. 213). And in spite of Littlechild's optimism, RPI−X is not as simple as he claimed. In all cases except that of BT, the formula has been more complex, with other costs passed through. In addition, regulators have been forced to consider the implications for other aspects: investment, quality, and innovation.

What is more, though Littlechild predicted that regulation would mostly be concerned with price review, in most industries the chief preoccupation has been with competition. More fundamentally, regulation has become not purely economic but also contains elements of social and environmental policy, as the succeeding chapters will show. The RPI − X formula has had to co-exist with the cross-subsidies which had been part of the *raison d'être* of the Morrisonian corporation.

In one of their articles, Beesley and Littlechild wrote 'Each act of privatization must be part of a whole scheme tailored to the particular conditions of each industry' (Beesley and Littlechild, 1983). In the event, political pressures of all kinds, from the dominant position of the men in charge of the industries to the date of the next general election and the prime minister's predilection for nuclear power meant that this excellent piece of advice was not followed.

The new system deliberately removed the regulation of utilities from government departments. The main intention was to depoliticize such decisions and to get away from the discredited methods, which had been used to control the nationalized industries. Originally it was hoped that Sir Gordon Borrie, Director General of Fair Trading, would regulate BT once it was privatized. When he declined to do this, OFTEL was set up, designed in the image of the OFT. In their turn the gas, electricity and water industries were each provided with a regulatory office headed by a director general. The same format was later followed for the Rail Regulator (ORR), and the rail franchising director (OFRAF) and OFLOT, the Lottery regulator. The Civil Aviation Authority is the regulator for BAA. These offices shared some common ground with the Next Steps agencies such as the Child Support Agency (CSA) and the Benefits Agency (BA) whose activities were carried on at one remove from departmental ministers, though not from parliamentary scrutiny. Both types of agency are staffed largely by civil servants, but the heads of the CSA and BA for example, though in some cases quite well known as public figures, have the status of permanent secretaries. The powers exercised by DGs are in some senses more similar to those of ministers. This has been the focus of much criticism: 'new and potentially hugely powerful agencies without precedent in British administrative history' (Walker, 1990, p. 151). It has been alleged that they are more powerful than ministers under the old system and have in effect been handed 'the stewardship of whole industries' (Bishop et al., 1995, p. 15).

The terms and conditions under which the regulators work are designed to insulate them from political pressure and also to keep them at arm's length from the industries they regulate to avoid the problem of 'agency capture'[1] which is a great concern in the US. This was also a cause for anxiety in the UK with regard to the nationalized industries. Indeed, avoidance of problems experienced on the other side of the Atlantic is an important leitmotiv in the story of how the British regulatory system was designed. The model is basically a non-participatory one. There were no public hearings in the early years and the regulator, having consulted with the firms concerned, was not obliged to give reasons for his decisions. This made them less open to the possibility of judicial review, another aspect of the American system that did not appeal to the British reformers.

The discretion allowed to the regulator is, it can be argued, the counterbalance to the inescapable problem of this kind of regulation: the fact that she or he can never have as much information about the company as the company has about itself. This 'information asymmetry' is a serious difficulty and not just a theoretical one. In the early years of the privatization of BG, for example, Sir Denis Rooke refused point blank to give the gas regulator information which he requested (Chapman, 1990, p. 125). A second example is the situation faced by Littlechild after the REC review in the summer of 1994, when a takeover bid for Northern Electric revealed new information about the RECs financial position. But it is also felt by some commentators (Veljanovski, 1994) that though a certain amount of discretion to determine the law and indeed to implement general rules is all right, the capability to modify licences gives the regulator undue power to force changes without allowing an input to other parties.

Accountability and its problems

As mentioned earlier, accountability was already controversial even in the days of nationalization. Under the new system, the deliberately distanced relation between regulator and government means that lines of accountability are unclear. Parliamentary scrutiny, as in former times, is eagerly pursued and several select committees notably the Trade and Industry Committee and the Public Accounts Committee have conducted enthusiastic enquiries into all aspects of the regulation of utilities. Political pressure can certainly be exerted and controversies aired by such means, as was shown at the time of the pit closure row in the autumn of 1992. This particular argument prompted the understandable comment that politicians seem to 'see the regulator as yet another part of the government which can be manipulated or pressured to take action' (Veljanovski, 1994, p. 6). Furthermore, regulators may be under great pressure to intervene before the set period is over if profits are very high, consumers are dissatisfied or a supplier is disadvantaged (Price, 1994a, p. 80).

There is no doubt that this has happened from time to time. Today's pressures may be subtler than the lunchtime directive, but they undoubtedly exist. But it is worth making the point that although theoretically and in some sense in practice separated from ministers and Whitehall, the regulators are also part of the pattern of networks which influence public policy decisions. In addition, they are also relatively well known public figures, 'public players' (Walker, 1990, p. 132) and part of the infinite series of pressures and counter pressures. They know each other, in some cases well, and perhaps constitute a network of their own. Littlechild's links with the IEA are of long standing. Carsberg, who advised Kenneth Baker on BT privatization and later became DG of OFTEL, went on to the OFT for a while and became a director of Cable and Wireless. Byatt, formerly an academic, became a Treasury economist (as was Spottiswoode), and was closely involved with the privatization programme before being appointed to Ofwat. Additionally, part of their duties is to advise government on policy towards their industries. Planning of the new windfall tax announced in July 1997 included input from the regulators, who attended many meetings with ministers and civil servants.

Thus, firmly connected to the political system, though not quite of it, the regulators are in a constitutional no man's land. They regulate the utilities on behalf of the government and the public. But their relation to the public is distant enough to create a problem of legitimacy that is exacerbated by the presence of another group – the shareholders. A further weakness of the system is in Ernsts's words: 'that the scope and strength of the regulatory regime is substantially dependent on the character, ethos and capacity of the DG' (Ernst, 1994, p. 181). In other words rather than being a few good men, the regulators may have their own agendas.

The third element in the new order of utility regulation was one largely unknown in the US, that of encouraging competition. This it seemed was a vital part of the intellectual foundation laid down by Littlechild, backed up by the IEA and favoured by more pragmatic influences like David Young. The ideal of a free market was supposedly one of the fundamental tenets of Thatcherism propounded by Nicholas Ridley and Keith Joseph. 'Competition', wrote Littlechild in his report on BT in 1983, 'is undisputedly the most effective means – perhaps ultimately the only effective means – of protecting consumers against monopoly power' (Foster, 1992, p. 205), and certainly infinitely preferable to regulation. And though his terms of reference stressed ensuring the maximum proceeds from the sale and facilitating BT's success as a commercial organization, the report also underlined the importance of competition as the main stimulus to efficiency.

When it came to the sale, however, the first privatization designed to have popular appeal, BT succeeded in avoiding dismemberment. Many of those involved in deciding the policy on regulation, including Nigel Lawson, Alan Walters and the Prime Minister herself had wanted the company broken up along regional lines as had happened to the US telephone system in 1984. But apparently solving the associated accounting problems would have taken two to three years to sort out and meant an unacceptable delay (Armstrong, Cowan and Vickers, 1994, p. 356n). Thoroughgoing liberalization as recommended first by Beesley and then by Littlechild was also avoided, since the government decided to licence the Mercury project and in November 1983 confirmed that the duopoly agreement, with Mercury limited to 3 per cent of the market, should continue until 1990. This was described by one commentator as a 'contest between a giant and a relative pygmy' (Burton, 1997, p. 168).

Clearly for the government, a successful sale and the transfer of ownership to the private sector were higher priorities than the introduction of competition, in spite of a statement by John Moore, then Financial Secretary to the Treasury, the same month: 'The long term success of the privatization programme will stand and fall by the extent to which it maximises competition' (Abromeit, 1988, p. 71).

The BT model was followed again for the gas industry and once more the industry proved powerful in its own defence. This was a much more controversial sale than that of BT, since being a more essential product, social considerations loomed larger. It was of this sale that Harold Macmillan made his famous remark about selling the family silver. The British Gas chairman, Sir Denis Rooke, supported by Peter Walker, the Secretary of State for Energy at the time, fiercely resisted a break up of the structure of the industry. Economic thinking once more yielded to political necessity – to achieve a successful sale and raise billions for the Treasury – making a trade off like BT, it has been suggested, between retaining the monopoly and moving into the private sector (Abromeit, 1988, pp. 75–6). It was also possible that, especially for a successful organization like British Gas, a move to the private sector would bring welcome relief from government interference. In the case of gas the technical expertise of those who ran the industry was a vital ingredient in the design of the regulatory system. Again there was haste; a need to get the deal done before the election which was due in 1987, so as to keep on side the 'Sids', the small shareholders, and ensure that BG stayed private.

The privatization of water was by far the most controversial, not to say unpopular (79 per cent opposed it, *Economist* 8 July 1989), of all the privatizations and the final bill for the extensive advertising campaign was £20 million. The difficulties of accommodating environmental as well as economic considerations resulted in a very slow progress from the earliest moves to final passage through parliament. Changes in 1983 intended to make water companies more business-like had reduced board sizes and excluded local authority members. All members were now appointed by the Secretary of State. The arrival of this item on the political agenda was prompted by the refusal of the chairman of Thames Water to increase charges by ten per cent to comply with a Treasury demand for £40 million. A Conservative backbench revolt was threatened; and a government minister, perhaps prompted by Nigel Lawson, indicated that a radical change was possible. This was, apparently, a political reaction to a political problem. The BT sale had been a success and British Gas was on its way to the market, but BA's flotation had had to be postponed, and the government was keen to 'keep the ball rolling'. The first White Paper in February 1986 produced a negative reaction from all interested groups because the ten Regional Water Authorities set up in 1974 were to be transferred to the private sector with a whole array of regulatory functions; they would be gamekeepers as well as poachers. In the face of massive opposition, including the possibility of a legal challenge from the Council for the Preservation of Rural England (CPRE), the plan was withdrawn and no further proposals were made till the eve of the 1987 election, when without any consultation, the Secretary of State Nicholas Ridley, arch opponent of the nationalized industries, came up with the idea of the National Rivers Authority (later to become part of the Environment Agency) as the regulator. The delay had allowed the chairmen to come round to the idea. After a year of work the Water Authorities Association managed to make common cause with Ridley and the bill finally became law in 1989.

By the time electricity privatization was reached, the determination to restructure was greater. The 1988 White paper was the first to commit to introducing an element of competition. Advice leaned towards five or more generating companies. But because the City had doubts about introducing competition and about the rising costs of dealing with old nuclear power stations, a lop-sided duopoly was eventually set up, with the larger of the two firms, National Power, judged able to take on all the nuclear risks. The national grid was to be taken from the CEGB and given to the twelve regional electricity companies (RECs). The chairman of the CEGB, Walter Marshall was opposed to a break up and in the end resigned over the question of the nuclear stations. But anxieties about the success of the flotation ultimately led to the nuclear sector being withdrawn from the sale by the Energy Secretary, Cecil Parkinson.

The result was an electricity supply industry like no other; 'a triumph of market structure over market forces' was one comment (Parker, 1993, p. 32). Its extreme complexity was partly due to technical issues, the near impossibility of storage and the need for supply and demand to be constantly in balance, partly to the problems of nuclear power and of the coal industry and partly to the desire to avoid another monolithic utility. But the retention of the strange duopoly once nuclear was no longer part of the deal was due to a reluctance to enact new legislation which might have brought the sale too close to the next general election. And though the legislation made an attempt to promote competition, a major preoccupation of the regulator subsequently was to try to increase this.

Political and economic views on the regulation of monopoly and what can be sold off have changed considerably since then. Industries or sections of industries previously thought unsaleable have been sold off; for instance the National Grid Company (NGC) was floated in December 1995 as was British Energy, created out of Nuclear Electric and Scottish Nuclear, in June 1996. A clear distinction is now perceived between the availability of a network, whether wires or pipes, and the supply of services through them. Equal access by suppliers is vital for competition; this means problems for the incumbent supplier and close involvement by the regulator, 'producing an intimacy which was not part of the initial philosophy of arm's length regulation' (Price, 1994b, p. 148).

As we shall see, privatization did not remove the utilities from the political arena. Nor does regulation, predicted by Littlechild to be a temporary phenomenon which would 'hold the fort' until competition arrived, show any sign of withering away. Though one of the chief justifications of the policy was the widening of consumer choice, it was developed with little public debate. The legislation was not in all cases fully discussed, and major parts of the new arrangements were not included in the acts but added afterwards. There were few White Papers and no public enquiries. The telecoms White Paper issued by the DTI in 1992 devoted barely a paragraph to OFTEL. 'Behind closed doors the value for X was decided by a cabal of government officials and representatives of the monopoly to be regulated' (Foster, 1992, p. 272). It is only in the ensuing years that the consumer has come to the fore and that the regulators have turned their attention to them.

A retrospective view of these industries at the beginning of the new century reveals how much, a great deal of it unforeseen, has changed since each of them was sold off. The old monopolies are scarcely recognisable. Unfamiliar names have appeared: Centrica, Hyder, Viridian. Vertical integration, multi-utilities, diversification, divestment and internationalization have resulted in a state of affairs far more complex than had been contemplated in the mid-1980s. Not surprisingly perhaps, controversy over how these industries should be regulated and managed has been almost continuous.

In telecoms, gas and electricity the structure of the industries has undergone a remarkable measure of change; even the water industry in which competition was still little better than embryonic has had its share of consolidation. Technical change had driven the telecom-munications industry and though BT retains the largest share of the domestic market, the growth of the mobile phone market and new commercial developments in data transfer and internet communications have brought in many other substantial companies. Regulation has become rather less interventionist; although a new price control was set for 2001. But, and this was to be a feature of gas, electricity and water as well, social obligations have become increasingly important.

The once vast and powerful coal industry, formerly the mainstay of the electricity supply industry, had been sold off in 1994, its decline accelerated as a result of the dash for gas which was beginning at the time of electricity privatization. Governments of both persuasions had, for political reasons, persisted in trying to slow down that decline by a series of measures which were largely unsuccessful and distorted the markets for both coal and gas and were later to endanger the Kyoto emission targets.

Competition, gradually introduced in the domestic gas market from early 1996 and electricity market from spring 1998, added further complexities to an already complicated situation. The huge British Gas company, after many battles in the MMC, was finally split in two in 1997. Centrica, the name deliberately chosen for being as empty of meaning as possible, was by 1999 a top ten FTSE performer and as competition in the domestic energy markets became established, had metamorphosed into an all purpose supplier of domestic services. It now provided insurance, home security and credit cards, as well as electricity and gas. Its acquisition of the Automobile Association (AA) gave it a customer base of 17 million and the company was also expanding into telecoms. The 1999 price cap was intended to be the last. As the only company to offer 'dual fuel' deals on a national scale, it was perhaps stronger than ever.

The structure of the electricity industry had changed almost beyond recognition. As a result of its fragmented structure, takeovers became an important issue for the regulator, the government and the MMC. The two original principal privatized generators, National Power and PowerGen had been joined by British Energy. The government's golden shares in the RECs expired in March 1995 and, looking ahead to competition in 1998, other companies joined in a scramble to buy them. By 1998 eight of the original twelve RECs were owned by US companies, several of which later thought better of their investments. Attempts by the two large generators to do the same were blocked by the Conservative government, against the recommendation of the MMC. The reason for this was apparently that competition in the industry was not sufficiently well developed. But vertical integration was not ruled out in principle; Scottish Power had been allowed to merge with Manweb; and Eastern, negotiating to buy power stations that the big generators were forced to sell, would also become vertically integrated. Once Labour had come to power in 1997, PowerGen was permitted to buy East Midlands Electricity from Dominion Resources; and National Power was allowed to acquire the supply business of Birmingham-based Midlands Electricity, also US owned – on condition they disposed of large power stations. British Energy also got a REC in 1999 – the supply side of SWALEC, previously part of the Welsh water and electricity company, Hyder. The expansionary publicly owned French electricity generator Electricite de France (EdF) had snatched London Electricity from under the nose of British Energy and went on to capture Sweb, becoming the largest player in the British electricity supply industry. Each generator now owned a supply business. In 1998 Scottish Hydro merged with Southern Electric. Thus with several vertically integrated power companies, the electricity supply industry looked entirely different from a decade before.

From April 2000 price control for direct debit customers was ended and the price cap for other customers was due to be removed in 2001.

In water, French privately owned companies had also made some inroads. They had bought several small water only companies in the early days of privatization, but Northumbrian in 1995 was the first purchase of a water and sewerage company; Lyonnaise des Eaux was the buyer. MidKent, after an MMC enquiry, was also taken over by a French utility. North West Water also bought Norweb electricity and Welsh Water acquired Swalec; these constituted the first regional multi-utilities. Scottish Power created a long-distance multi-utility when it successfully bid for Southern Water in 1996.

This rash of takeover and merger attempts both established the MMC as 'the regulator of last resort' (Armstrong et al., 1994, p. 169), since many of them were referred to it, and at the same time revealed the Conservative government's lack of a policy for the utilities, since the decisions on whether to have an enquiry or whether to accept the Commission's recommendations had no consistency about them.

It was not only the battles for corporate control that kept the privatized utilities in the news. There was also the severe problem in maintaining supply experienced by Yorkshire Water in the very dry summer of 1995 and in the same year the decision of the electricity regulator Stephen Littlechild to revisit his distribution price review. All of this resulted in what has been described as 'a real crisis of regulatory legitimacy' (Prosser, 1997, p. 179). Public opinion, never favourable to privatization grew increasingly antagonistic. The approach of a general election, however, and attempts to place greater emphasis on the concerns of consumers, accompanied by the beginning of price benefits, made for a change in the climate of opinion.

The Labour party which had vehemently opposed privatization had begun to position itself to accept the status quo when, under John Smith's leadership, it developed the idea of a windfall tax, which would be used to finance a New Deal for the young unemployed. Though this was the only definite commitment the party made on the utilities, it was clear by 1995 once Blair had become leader, that renationalization was not an option and that if elected Labour would emphasise consumer interests and environmental issues in any reforms. It was also widely expected that the two regulatory offices for electricity and gas would be merged into one with probable benefits for an overall energy policy. This amalgamation did in fact take place in 1999. Clearer guidance for the regulators from the government was also promised. This was implicitly criticized by Ian Byatt in September 1999 when he emphasised the success of arms' length regulation. How far this would go remained unclear, but questions of accountability will remain. What we have is a system which, now is so much more transparent than under nationalization and indeed than it was fifteen years ago, is subject to pressures from all sides. Conflicts of interest are endemic; making special cases of particular classes of consumers does not accord with competition. Lowering energy prices can endanger environmental progress. High standards of water quality and lower water bills may not both be possible. As the succeeding chapters will show the system is one replete with such incompatibilities and in which accountability is frequently, if not always, imperfect. The new Utilities Act aimed to provide 'clearer guidelines' for regulators, but these may raise as many problems as they solve.

2
Regulators at Work

'Regulation is a business in which people can make a difference.'*

It was an irony of the Thatcher government's privatization programme that deregulation brought with it so much new regulation. Implementation and enforcement of the regulation of utilities unusually for the UK was placed in the hands of single individuals, on whom were bestowed extensive powers. OFTEL and the other offices that followed for gas, electricity and water are non-ministerial departments. In each case there is a Secretary of State responsible for appointing the regulator and issuing licences. This means that their accountability as generally understood in the British system is by no means straightforward. Indeed they have been described as 'constitutional anomalies' (Veljanovski, 1991, p. 16). There is a curious hybrid quality about the regulators, as also perhaps about their City counterparts. In some respects they resemble civil servants, but in others they are more like ministers and though neither civil servants nor politicians, they require some of the qualities of both. They are public figures, up to a point; they have a certain expertise, something rather unusual in British public life, indeed their expertise is argued by some to bestow on them their legitimacy (Prosser, 1997, p. 16). They give press conferences and appear before Select Committees of the House of Commons. They fight for their budgets like ministers. They are not elected as some US regulators are, but appointed for a period of five years or more and removal from office is very difficult.[1] However, unlike either civil servant or politician, a regulator is legally accountable.

*Irvine Stelzer, OXREP 1988.

"

These 'high priests of public policy' (Hansard, Commons, Session 1994–5, vol. 260, col. 88–90) have in the past ten to fifteen years become almost household names, though less notorious than the directors of privatized companies characterized as 'fat cats'. More modestly remunerated and acting in many ways as intermediaries, the regulators occupy a pivotal position. To the regulated firms they represent both the government and the consumers. To the government, they act as go-betweens, ostensibly independent, though one of their roles is as adviser to the Secretary of State and sometimes they do the government's bidding. To the public they resemble referees or umpires and are responsible for getting a fair deal from the utilities. So, quite apart from the complex technical and accounting issues with which they must deal, the regulators have a demanding role as arbiters, negotiators and mediators between consumers and producers.

Their independence from government, and therefore, ostensibly, from politics, is at once an advantage and a disadvantage. To retain credibility for the office and for the government they must remain at arms' length from Whitehall; they are watchdogs not poodles. But if the system is to be judged a success, they must also try and achieve public legitimacy and the original legislation gave little support to this, since it mostly endorsed the discretion of the regulator. Perceived expertise and effectiveness as well as accountability are necessary for such legitimacy. They will only be demonstrated by means of open procedures; transparency, or 'sunshine regulation' as it has been called, is the only route to complete public acceptance. To the extent that the regulators are publicly available, providing as one commentator put it 'accountability by availability' (Walker, 1990, p. 152), and that the system is an adversarial one, they are players in a game of pressure group politics. Accountability is a theme that will recur throughout the succeeding chapters. Anxiety about its being fulfilled in this area is based on three reservations about the system as it has been set up. First, not only do their duties sometimes conflict, the discretion granted to them is wide; they are to exercise their powers 'in the manner…best calculated' to fulfil them (Prosser, 1997, p. 52; Thatcher, 1998, p. 126). Secondly there is the personalisation that has characterized the conduct of regulation for most of the first decade and a half of its practice. Thirdly, the line of responsibility between the regulators, and other agencies and government departments is ill defined; there is a lack of clarity about the regulators' objectives and to whom precisely they are accountable.

All three regulators – four before electricity and gas regulation were united in Ofgem – had a very similar range of duties and responsibilities though there were variations of detail. The primary one was to ensure that supply met all reasonable demands, then that the suppliers should be able to finance the provision of the service, and to promote competition. Secondary duties included protecting the interests of consumers, the promotion of efficiency and economy, ensuring safety, promoting research and development. There were also duties to protect the environment and have regard to the needs of particular groups such as the sick, disabled, those in rural areas and pensioners. The same duties were also laid on the Secretary of State. The breadth of the wording and the fact that economic and social issues were jumbled together without much heed as to whether they were mutually compatible was just the beginning. Wider aims, such as the public interest, received no mention.

These were the duties imposed by the privatization acts, but various aspects of competition policy also applied to the utilities and the Director General of Fair Trading and the Competition Commission (formerly the Monopolies and Mergers Commission or MMC) also have jurisdiction in certain circumstances. These will be dealt with later, but it is already plain that the duties and obligations of the regulators raise many complex questions.

This very general job description has been clarified over time and priorities have been established. The extension of competition as the best way to offer lower prices and more choice has become the top priority, apart from the water industry, where genuine competition is still on a small scale. The RPI $-$ X price cap, plus other price constraints, have provided incentives to cut costs and improve efficiency. Prices have fallen. Regulators have tried to get prices to reflect costs more closely, and have also set limits on rates of return on capital earned by the companies. Gradually an idea of what is an appropriate return on investment has begun to be developed (PAC, Session 1996–7, HC 89). Over the years, the consumer has become more important in the regulators' thinking and great efforts have been made to improve quality, as well as the insistence on social obligations.

Clearly, however, these duties and functions contain contradictions. For instance, the protection of particular groups of consumers is not compatible with full-blown competition, since it is achieved by means of cross-subsidy. Social issues such as these it is argued, are a matter for governmental decision. Other duties such as the obligation to protect the environment are so vague as not to be meaningful. As a result, the individuals concerned have had to interpret their role, developing the idea of a regulator and what he or she should do. Equally problematic, it could be argued, is the lack of transparency that, though now much less marked, has been the hallmark of much of the short history of these innovative public offices. There was no general duty to provide explanations. This was widely criticized, especially by the various parliamentary select committees that have examined the issue (Trade and Industry Committee, 1992–3 (HC 237), 1994–5 (HC 481), 1996–7 (HC 50)). Judicial review, possible in theory but rarely resorted to, especially in the early years, is much more difficult if reasons are not given. The 1995 Gas Act included a provision that the gas regulator should give reasons and there was pressure to apply this to electricity as well. Consumer bodies such as the National Consumers Council (NCC) and the Consumers Association (CA) and also the industries' own consumer organizations all press constantly for greater openness. From the point of view of the public this is probably just as important as the formal if obscure lines of accountability via the Secretary of State, parliament, the Public Accounts Committee, the National Audit Office and the annual report.

The regulators: who are they?

As noted in the previous chapter, if not exactly brought into being in a fit of absence of mind (Walker, 1990, p. 150), the new system was not planned in great detail in advance. Privatization may have been part of the Conservative party's ideological baggage and well entrenched in the successive manifestos, as Nigel Lawson claims (Lawson, 1992, p. 199), but the regulation of monopoly utilities once privatized had no worked out rationale apart from the work of Professor Littlechild on RPI − X price control. The system has evolved in a piecemeal fashion from two basic elements. The first was an office with an independent regulator, based on the Office of Fair Trading (OFT), a product of the Heath administration in 1973. The second was the price cap formula, the 'philosopher's stone' of regulation (TIC, Session 1996–7, HC 50, Memos, p. 135). The rest the regulators had to make up as they went along.

By the turn of the century, eight individuals had filled the posts at OFTEL, Ofwat, OFFER and Ofgas (now Ofgem). Academics and civil servants dominated the cast list. The first, Sir Bryan Carsberg of OFTEL had been a professor of accounting and later moved on to the OFT, to take over from Sir Gordon Borrie, who had held the post for sixteen years. The much criticized cult of personality which has been indulged in by several of the Directors General is said to have started with Sir Gordon, and been continued by Sir Bryan Carsberg. The OFT had the reputation of being very media conscious. Carsberg's successor at

OFTEL, Don Cruickshank was a departure from the academic tendency. Michael Heseltine, who as President of the Board of Trade had the appointment in his gift, made it clear that he was seeking a person who had 'hands on' experience of running a company in a competitive environment. Cruickshank had worked at McKinsey, in broadcasting and entertainment and airlines as managing director of the Virgin Group, where he had helped to break monopolies, but came from a public sector job as Chief Executive of the NHS in Scotland and was noted for his 'fastidious attention to detail' (*Times*, 26 Jan. 1999). Cruickshank was much praised for his defence of the consumer; tough, fair and consistent, his relations with BT were often very cool and his style fairly autocratic (Scott et al., 1997). OFTEL, 'in law a body without teeth', had under the direction of these two men become an organization whose influence exceeded its formal powers because it had the resources to deal with a wide range of regulatory issues and because of Carsberg's influence (Beesley and Laidlaw, 1995, p. 319). BT's fear of an MMC referral that might lead to a recommendation to split the company made OFTEL very powerful. It gradually increased its coverage of BT business and succeeded in making telecommunications a competitive industry in spite of increasingly strong social obligations.

David Edmonds succeeded Cruickshank in March 1998. Formerly with Natwest, he had previously spent years as a civil servant and then become chief executive of the Housing Corporation and chairman of the charity Crisis. Margaret Beckett, secretary of state at the DTI at the time, said she had chosen him because she wanted to appoint someone with 'direct experience of managing significant change' (*Financial Times*, 24 March 1998), but his commercial experience seemed limited and he had no prior knowledge of telecoms.

The first Director General of Gas Supply, Sir James McKinnon, came like Carsberg, from a business background. He was also an accountant by training and joined Ofgas from the Imperial Group where he had been finance director. He had contributed much to the improvement of financial reporting and had doubtless met Carsberg on committees dealing with accountancy matters. Again like Carsberg, he was accused of self-promotion and regulation by press release. He acquired a reputation for being aggressive and difficult. This was also the reputation of Sir Denis Rooke, the chairman of British Gas who famously told his staff that nothing would change on privatization. Relations between the two were acrimonious in the extreme and seem to have set a pattern for future relations between the regulator and the industry. But McKinnon had made a start in dismantling the monolithic company and embarking on the slow transition to a competitive gas industry. He was not averse to publicity, even appearing one Christmas in a Santa Claus suit. Perhaps he hoped that this might counteract the unfortunate impression that, according to him had been received by many, that his office was concerned with gas disconnection! (Foster, 1992, p. 255).

McKinnon's successor, Clare Spottiswoode also claimed a business background but a more accurate description would be a Treasury economist. She strongly favoured competition in the domestic market at a time when it was widely thought that such a reform would result in higher prices. Though later proved right on this, her approach was generally seen as too academic and widely regarded as too 'Austrian'[2] in her views (Prosser, 1997, p. 97). She was most notorious for her refusal to sanction the levy on gas customers for the Energy Saving Trust (EST), a story told in Chapter 7.

Academic economists are as numerous as accountants in this area of activity. Ian Byatt, the water regulator, was an LSE lecturer early in his career, as was Sir Bryan Carsberg. Byatt then had a variety of civil service jobs before becoming deputy chief economic adviser at the Treasury from 1978 to 1989, when he became closely involved in the finances of the nationalized industries, especially on rate of return. If there is some truth in the remark that 'Water regulation is a new form of administration rather than a regulatory regime for a commercial activity' (Foster, 1992, p. 409), Byatt's appointment seems a most appropriate one. Competition in water, though now beginning to develop, was at the outset seen as all but impossible. Against this background, a senior civil servant such as Ian Byatt, well versed in the obscure details of rate of return in nationalized industries and the niceties of how things are done in Whitehall, seemed eminently suitable.

Stephen Littlechild, the first electricity regulator, whose other activities in connection with the Conservative privatization programme were detailed in the first chapter, also lectured, not at the LSE, but at Birmingham University. He became a member of the MMC in 1983 and was a member of the panel which undertook the 1987–8 enquiry into British Gas.

These people practically form a policy network of their own, together with a few others, like civil servants Eileen Marshall and Penny Boys, both of whom worked in the Department of Energy. Dr Marshall, a former student of Littlechild, worked first at OFFER and then moved to Ofgas, continuing to do a day a week at the electricity regulator; later she was appointed to conduct the enquiry into the workings of the electricity pool[3] and became a deputy director general at Ofgem. Ms Boys went to the MMC as its secretary. The world of utility regulation is a small one: the 1996 report by the NAO on the regulators made use of, as is quite usual, a panel of advisers. They included Sir Christopher Foster, who had been as a senior partner of Coopers and Lybrand, closely involved in the planning of the privatized electricity industry, and was memorably described by Simon Jenkins as 'Thatcherisms's Doctor Strangelove' (Jenkins, 1996, p. 53); John Kay of consultancy London Economics and respected writer on regulation; and three people from large well known firms of accountants/management consultants. In other words no one who was not an academic or a consultant. This is a fairly closed circle.

One of the chief criticisms of the privatized utilities over the first five to ten years was of the inappropriateness of having two separate regulators for electricity and gas. As gas was increasingly used for power generation from the early 1990s, the substitutability of the two became even greater than before. These developments and those in the power-generating sector, as will be seen, had a major impact on the coal industry and serious political repercussions. As a result, the first electricity regulator found himself under attack on several occasions for his failure to act on more general energy policy issues. The amalgamation of the two offices was part of the Labour party's proposed reforms; and as first Spottiswoode's and then Littlechild's contracts came to an end, at the end of 1998 and 1999 respectively, Callum McCarthy took over responsibility for both. An economist like so many of his colleagues past and present, the new director general of Ofgem, as it was eventually named, was a civil servant at the time of the early sales of public sector assets. He had also been private secretary to Roy Hattersley and Norman Tebbit, so gained valuable political awareness. He left Whitehall to work in the City and also worked for Barclays Bank in the Far East and USA. Well connected with the new Labour hierarchy, his style was robust, if not confrontational. He seemed to relish the high profile nature of the appointment.

He soon announced a new structure and a London location for the new office; electricity and gas would be dealt with on an integrated basis, with clear lines of responsibility and an advisory board. This was not an entirely new idea; all the regulators had from time to time appointed outside advisers. The Ofgem board was a little different, however since it included Lord Borrie, formerly of the OFT, and Lord Currie of London Business School, both newly created Labour life peers. (Also included were Gill Owen of the Public Utilities Access Forum (PUAF), Nigel Rudd of Williams Holdings and East Midlands

Electricity and a senior accountant from Touche Ross.) There was some criticism of the life peers' presence since their political allegiance was clear. McCarthy's response was that there was a relatively small pool of suitable board members and that though he knew them both, they passed his 'Christmas card test' – he did not send them one, nor they him presumably.

Resources and staffing

The resources, especially human resources, of the regulators are quite limited. In the early days the Ofgas complement of staff was usually below thirty, though The *Economist's* description of it as a 'regulatory dwarf' (12 Oct. 1986) did not refer to its size but its powers. By 1995 the numbers had grown to a total of 86. The small staff size, partly due to the fact that the Gas Consumers Council was a separate organization, might have been responsible though for the spectacular changes of mind that took place. All the offices have grown but they remain small compared with the companies they regulate. Ian Byatt commented that each of the 30 or so water companies that he was supposed to be supervising would have a regulatory staff at least as big as his. In 1996 the total was 178 permanent staff including some working in the regional consumer service committees and the annual staff turnover was 25 per cent; not surprisingly, he reported to the NAO that in order to do the job properly he needed more resources. By 2000 this had increased to 233, of which a quarter were based in the regional offices of the Customer Service Committees and turnover was down to only 14 per cent.

In common with the OFT, many of the staff in the regulators' offices come from the civil service, and are often in defined civil service grades and functions. In the past, most OFTEL staff for instance were on loan from different departments or agencies, though in 1993 it took on responsibility for its own human resources function from the DTI and began recruiting more widely. Like Ofwat, OFTEL had a high staff turnover; 39 per cent left in 1997. From 1997 OFTEL was able to set its own pay scales and offer variable salaries, but half were still from civil service posts, usually the DTI and often returned there (Hall et al., 2000, p. 36). They encouraged secondment, and in 1996 at the time of the NAO report had six members of staff seconded from solicitors. In 1999 there were about 195 staff. All the offices occasionally recruited from the industries they regulate and vice versa. This can happen at the highest levels. Chris Bolt, Regulation Director at Transco, previously worked at Ofwat, OFFER and the Office of the Rail Regulator. Ofgem got off to an uncertain start when the OFFER employees refused to move to the capital. Only 30 of 100 staff were prepared to go. Ofgem had around 125 staff at the end of 1999 but was in great need of more personnel to replace those who had not moved to London from Birmingham with the office, and to arrive at the right mix of skills. A greater use of consultants was needed to compensate for shortages. In general, staff at the regulators' offices are criticized as not professional enough; civil service rates of pay are perhaps inadequate to attract the best from outside with wider experience. Inadequate levels and calibre of staffing could lead to capture and also in effect increase the difficulty of entry by new suppliers. The Trade and Industry Select Committee enquiry into energy regulation in 1997 heard evidence from many witnesses to this effect; it was quite widely thought that there was an unbalanced mix of staff, dominated by academic economists, and a lack of competence in accountancy. What was required, according to some, was some 'hard nosed accountants from the private sector' who could read a balance sheet and take the companies apart rather than indulge the finer points of CCA accounting (TIC 1997, Memoranda p. 134). This view was clearly shared by City observers, who gave high priority to vigorous financial analysis (Hawkins, 1994, p. 159). Detailed information on staffing is hard to get at, partly because people are not always doing jobs related to their qualifications. The tendency is often to promote and transfer from within even if the skills do not match exactly, because specialised knowledge of the industry is such a large part of any job. Financial resources have to be fought for from the Treasury like other departments. Net expenditures in 1994–5 totalled £33 million. OFTEL, Ofwat and OFFER all spent in the region of £9 million but Ofgas less than half that. These sums were roughly equivalent to what was charged in licence fees. In 1999–2000 Ofgem spent four times this, excluding the cost of the merger of the two offices and the new electricity trading arrangements.

With such small staffs, mostly non-specialist, the regulators have of necessity brought in consultants to help with price reviews etc. This has been criticized on various grounds, but consultants have been closely involved with privatization and regulation – they were 'present at the creation'[4] – to purloin a phrase borrowed by Nigel Lawson in his account of the privatization process. Management consultancy began to permeate Whitehall almost from the earliest Thatcher years. Lawson himself, when Energy Minister, privately employed Sir Christopher Foster and Lord Chorley of Coopers and Lybrand to examine the question of electricity privatization (Lawson, 1992, p. 179).

Innovations such as the Financial Management Initiative (FMI) in 1982 brought management consultants into government on a much larger scale than before. The spread of management information systems and management accounting systems brought work for them and began a movement of civil servants, now being much more richly rewarded, in the opposite direction. Privatization increased this demand by many times. Between 1989 and 1993 the number of people leaving Whitehall for consultancy increased by a factor of three and preparation for privatization required large amounts of manpower. To take the electricity industry as an example, Price Waterhouse were appointed in 1987 to review options for its future structure. This led to the 1988 White Paper and the firm subsequently became advisers to the twelve RECs and consequently had a good deal of influence on the framework for regulation, capital structure, accounting, and the electricity pool (Ward, 1993, p. 304). Littlechild was of course also involved in this process. A similar sequence of events took place with the other privatizations. Financial advisers also had a good deal of input as they were writing prospectuses.

Consultants of all kinds are used for a wide range of tasks. They provide expertise and advice on economics, project management, corporate finance, accountancy, technical and engineering issues, legal matters, consumer affairs, market research. OFTEL sees consultancy as important and keeps Ernst and Young and Touche Ross on stand-by contracts. Touche Ross also handled the day-to-day management of the 1997 transportation and storage review for Ofgas. In addition Coopers and Lybrand did an efficiency study of operational expenditure (Prosser, 1997, p. 99). This study and another on capital expenditure resulted in savage cuts by Ofgas and a violent reaction from BG. Ofwat also uses consultants. KPMG in 1990 considered the options for the next review on its behalf. But because it was decided to spread the review over a longer period of time, not just one year, it was possible to do more of the work in house and therefore be less dependent on consultants. They are used however, on City matters, for project management and for specific studies, employing both engineers and academics.

Consultants can also reinforce bureaucracy particularly in the water industry. During the 1999 price review, companies had to submit a mass of detailed information to Ofwat, all of which had to be audited by company 'reporters' (who are also management consultants). A further layer of auditing was added: two further sets of management consultants, including KPMG, were employed to report on the reporters. Their remit included examination of the relationship between the reporters and the water companies and whether they were fulfilling their primary duty of care to the DG, Ian Byatt. Might this be described as a report too far? (*Utilities Journal*, March 1998, 'Reporting on the Reporters').

OFFER seemed to make less extensive use of outside consultants than the other regulators. They were used for price reviews, pool enquiries and other matters, such as collection of the Fossil Fuel Levy[5] which was contracted out to Coopers and Lybrand, who also did a report in July 1996 on competition and regulation. PA did some work on the 1998 competition project. KPMG did the ill-fated REC review of 1995, which was seriously criticized and will be examined in depth later in this chapter. OFFER also had an analyst on contract to report on City perceptions. Littlechild hired London Economics to do some work on the review of the RECs' economic purchasing requirements and was criticized in *The Times* for contracting out research to firms with past or present commercial connections to the regulated companies (5 Nov. 1992). But this is hard to avoid. Rothschilds were advising both the DTI and the RECs' at the time. Where Ofgas spent £2.9 million in 1996, OFFER spent only £1.3 million; but the latter had twice as many staff. In any case, expenditure varies from year to year depending on reviews, MMC referrals and so on. Some argue that the use of consultants is detrimental as well as expensive, others that they could bring much needed consistency across the utilities. Wherever the truth lies, it is hard to disagree with Madsen Pirie of the Adam Smith Institute that policy formulation itself has been privatized (Ward, 1993, p. 305).

External advisers do not have to be management consultants. Regulators often have academic backup, for example Professor Martin Cave is a part time adviser to OFTEL. People from businesses of all kinds are also used. Sir Nigel Rudd, later to join Ofgem's advisory board and the late Professor Michael Beesley both advised Ofgas during the 1996–7 MMC enquiry. Littlechild had three senior businessmen advising him in 1996 and Ofwat appointed five industrialists in early 1998 for the periodic review. In 1999 McCarthy appointed a board to provide formal opinions in the case of taking action against electricity generators for abuse of market power. The members included a distinguished legal academic, three economists and Sir Bryan Carsberg (Ofgem press release 7 Dec. 1999).

Regulatory styles

Though the duties laid upon them are in essence very similar, the industries that the regulators supervise are very different in structure, maturity and technology. OFTEL and Ofgas were at the outset regulating a single, nationwide, monolithic industry, one increasingly 'hightech', the other rather the opposite. The electricity and water regulators, on the other hand, were overseeing a large number of companies. Ofwat has to regulate more than thirty regional water and sewerage (WASCs) or water only companies (WOCs). OFFER directed twelve RECs plus the two generating companies and the NGC. The water industry was in need of massive investment, while the electricity generation, distribution and supply industry was not, indeed there was some evidence of 'goldplating'.

Styles of regulation also vary greatly: the extent of transparency, the amount of consultation and the readiness to intervene have been very different. The manner in which the regulator treats its regulated companies, whether few or many, is obviously partly a question of personality, but the style of regulation is basically driven by the circumstances of the different industries (Vass, 1994b, p. 209). Sir James McKinnon's pugnacious and irritable style with British Gas, whose own chairman immediately after privatization, Sir Denis Rooke, was also fairly aggressive, may have been the most effective way to deal with a very large company set on continuing as before, but it also reflected his character.

Rooke, who had worked his way up from the bottom of British Gas over 37 years, had a low opinion of politicians and civil servants. He and his corporation saw its own interest and the national interest as being identical (Price, 1994c, p. 148). British Gas had a history of secretiveness; no performance indicators were available and when a report and accounts were published in 1986 it was for the first time in ten years. Rooke had insisted on maintaining the monolithic character of his organization after privatization and the government, in a hurry, had acceded to this. The Gas Act did everything possible to appease the British Gas chairman. There was no obligation to make public the monopoly profits and there was no regulation of industrial gas prices. The regulator had few weapons to counter Rooke's refusal to disclose information to Ofgas, but he began to suspect that the 2 per cent figure for X was too low. To make matters worse, senior management had given themselves salary increases approaching fifty per cent, a situation paralleled a few years later when Cedric Brown and his board raised their own salaries and at the same time sacked staff in gas showrooms. The dispute came into the open in July 1987, when Ofgas said it would take legal action if British Gas would not reveal its forecast for its average price. On the morning of the annual general meeting, the figures were delivered – but hostilities continued and a referral was made to the MMC on the grounds of price discrimination in the industrial market. The regulatory dwarf triumphed, and McKinnon, whatever his shortcomings, 'created a climate in which the reduction of British Gas' market share became inevitable' (Stern, 1994, pp. 32–3). This episode, though exhibiting more acrimony than most, illustrates the key problems in the relationship between regulator and regulated. Though personality can play a considerable part, it was more likely to be the case at the extreme, where the regulator faced a single national monopolist.

It would be a mistake, however, though different regulators have had their different methods of working, to see them as all-powerful individuals within their organizations. OFTEL under Don Cruickshank had a very particular style that included creating tension between the various departments and last minute changes in direction. It was nonetheless an organization in which the style of decision-making was frequently 'collegial' and 'regulatory functions were widely dispersed' including to junior staff (Scott et al., 1997, p. 246). This was true too of Ofwat in the 1999 review. Clare Spottiswoode apparently saw her role as 'like the chairman of a company' (PAC, Session 1996–7, para. 82). Callum McCarthy, on taking over the functions of both the gas and electricity regulators in 1999, in addition to the advisory board, purposefully assembled a team that had a range of responsibilities to whom he could delegate. This management committee included Richard Morse, like him a City man, to deal with regulation and price control, Eileen Marshall to take charge of supply chains and John Neilson, ex-DTI and Department of Energy and former PPS to the Energy Secretary 1989–92, to deal with customer issues. Each of these was a deputy director general.

One of the most striking changes in utility regulation since the early years is the shift towards greater transparency. Like accountability, transparency is one of the recurring themes of this study. Though much greater than under the old regime, there was until 2000 no general duty to consult, explain, or give reasons for decisions, though all regulators have moved in the direction of more public consultation, even holding meetings. Failure to provide reasons on the part of the electricity regulator was a particular cause for concern in the mid-1990s, though the government supported him. In later reviews, such as the National Grid Company (NGC), more consultation papers were issued and the whole process was more open than before, but Littlechild still fell short of the standards of openness demonstrated by his colleagues. Ofgas procedures were also less transparent than OFTEL or Ofwat since it would not permit BG access to the consultants' reports on Transco (Prosser, 1997, pp. 115 and 178). The other regulators have held public seminars, at which key issues have been discussed. OFTEL led the way with public meetings in February 1995 and holds them regularly to discuss plans and targets for the next two years (*Times*, 31 Dec. 1997). Rulings on disputes between parties are also published but there is less transparency on decision making.

At Ofwat, Ian Byatt was always committed to a transparent approach, whereas the first electricity regulator was much less likely to be generous about the amount of information that is released. However, the root cause of this contrast is much more likely to be that in an industry in which the prospects for competition are pretty small, commercial confidentiality is not a major consideration. As Byatt once said, 'Water is an industry little touched by economics' (Byatt, 1996, p. 63). Littlechild's style, which no doubt reflected his personality as well as his economic views, was to be much more distant from his companies than Byatt from his.

Byatt again was exceptionally keen to consult ministers, to obtain guidelines from them, for instance on water quality where the law could offer no guidance and to admit that there was of necessity 'a great deal of art as well as science' in his job (Byatt, 1994, p. 35). He clearly sees the limits of economics: being water regulator is an exercise in the art of the possible. But for the other regulators too, 'regulation is also rooted in politics, involving the interaction of power plays, between dominant groups within society...(the transition to) more fragmentary competitive markets complicates the regulatory process and reduces the regulators' capacity to apply economic theory... [a regulator is] a resolver of problems with a lot of data missing and tremendous ambiguity of objectives' (Lapsley and Kilpatrick, 1997, p. 56).

Byatt, a civil servant of many years standing, stressed the importance of good processes and again found little help from the legislation or the licence. His aim was to set up procedures which were not only transparent, but fair and defensible (Byatt, 1995, pp. 21–2), and to involve environmental groups and consumers as well as the companies. His efforts towards a more transparent regime thus included more consultation; an early example was the consultation paper *Paying for Water* (1990), an ambitious undertaking which tried to get in touch with a wide audience and used a video as well as conventional press releases. *Paying for Quality*, which came later (1993), was an open letter to the Secretaries of State for the Environment and Wales on the impact that the increasingly strict quality rules would have on customers' bills. This issue was a very serious one, since prices for water had risen far more than for other utilities, during the five years from

1989–90 to 1994–5 they rose 25 per cent in real terms – a big anxiety for Ofwat. Byatt's modus operandi demonstrated his skill as a political operator and exponent of public relations; his 'Dear M.D.' letters were unique. By including the Customer Service Committees (CSCs) in what became an evolutionary process his hand was strengthened in insisting on affordability (Prosser, 1997, p. 146), but ultimately he admitted that the government would always have the last word. Littlechild on the other hand, astonished the Trade and Industry Select Committee by the revelation that he had not met the President of the Board of Trade after a year in office (Prosser, 1997, p. 159).

By law the regulators must consult publicly before amending a licence, though all now consult more than this and see it as serving several purposes of their own. It can ensure that the office is aware of relevant considerations, can allow people to put forward their views, and enables the directors to set out their thinking on different issues. The regulators also all consult as part of a price review; for the 1994 reviews they all consulted early, Ofwat as mentioned taking three years, and keeping in contact with OFFER during the process. Their methods of operation remained rather different, however; since Byatt's declared aim was to 'make the decision system as transparent as possi-ble…and avoid surprises for all parties' (Rees, 1994, p. 62). OFTEL too has adopted very extensive consultation procedures and is concerned to come to an acceptable decision (Scott et al., 1997, p. 247).

Levels of intervention by regulators, in all cases more intensive than initially envisaged, have also varied widely. Ofwat has certainly been far more interventionist than the others in terms of price reviews. Initial price caps set in 1989 were due to last ten years, but in July 1991, Byatt announced he would review all price caps after five years. This was attacked as simply intrusive regulation. The regulator has been accused of yielding to pressure from political parties, customers, and organized groups, to the extent that the credibility of the price cap lasting for ten years had been destroyed (Helm, 1995, p. 34). In Byatt's defence it could be argued that a five year review was inevitable since the profits of the water industry were rising, more environmental directives were being issued by the EU and the regulator was acquiring more information (Vass, 1993a, p. 58). The same thing happened again in 1996 when the review due in 2004 was brought forward to 1999. Apart from this, however, Ofwat also intervened to increase obligations or to persuade companies not to put up charges by as much as the for-mula permitted (Helm, 1999). The water companies were a particular target of the Labour party when in opposition and indeed once in office put great pressure on the regulator to improve performance on leakages.

At the other end of the spectrum, in an industry much closer to having meaningful competition, at least in some respects, OFFER was reluctant to intervene even when under great pressure to do so. Though professing a laissez faire attitude, Littlechild was drawn in, especially to supervising the two major players in the generating sector, National Power and PowerGen, partly as a result of complaints from larger industrial customers led by the Energy Intensive Users Group. The electricity pool, a complex spot market in which the two large generators had considerable market power in spite of the entry of smaller generators, was the subject of several enquiries. Because they still had virtually all the marginal plant, the big two dominated and a sector which was supposed not to require regulation took up a considerable amount of OFFER's time. Ultimately it was decided to reform these arrangements and the pool was replaced by NETA.[6]

The gas industry was rather different: it was involved in a more or less continuous battle with its regulator from privatization right up till 1997, but mostly on structure rather than prices. Chapter 4 has an account of this. OFTEL has also been quite interventionist, often on detailed points, particularly perhaps on social obligations.

Relations between regulators and regulated companies

In general the main focus of regulator/company relations will be pricing of the goods and services supplied by the utilities. This is also naturally the principal concern of consumers, both domestic and industrial, though quality of service can become an overriding concern when problems arise; if the price constraint is binding, quality degradation is an obvious way to boost profit. As Chapter 1 explained, the original prices were set in secret, their levels dictated by political as much as economic considerations.

The resetting of X after five years is a matter of fine-tuning. Though in many ways highly technical, this process is likely to have strongly political overtones, if only in relation to the issue of how well shareholders seem to be faring in comparison with consumers. 'No formula' as Prosser states, 'can be immune from public and political pressure' (Prosser, 1997, p. 179). But the asymmetry of information between regulated and regulator turns the process into a strategic game in which the utility companies tend to hold the winning cards. The basis of the game is that the company always and inevitably knows more than the regulator does. The managers of the regulated utility have deep knowledge and experience of the technology, the market and the physical infrastructure of their industry, built up over many years. Though the companies are only a few years old in private sector terms, they are staffed for the most part by people who have been in the industry for a long time and know how it works. Since the objectives of the regulator and those of the company systematically conflict, the relationship is likely to be an adversarial one. The point of the RPI − X control is to make the company pass on to its customers some of its efficiency gains while simultaneously providing it with an incentive to reduce its costs. If it can reduce its costs by more than X it gets to keep the difference.

There is thus an incentive to exaggerate forecasts of operating costs and investment requirements and equally an incentive to present information selectively and produce business plans that may overstate costs and understate demand. This also has an effect on capital markets – financial analysts and consultants spend time modelling and attempting to predict how each director general will exercise his discretion (Helm, 1994a, p. 28). Inside the companies a similar process also takes place. The uncertainty creates speculation and affects the pricing of shares in utility companies.

From the company's point of view, as Kay points out, 'the rational response is to maintain a reserve of inefficiency', part of which may be cut out in the interval before the next regulatory review (Kay, 1996, p. 155). For the companies, success consists in doing better than the regulator had anticipated, while for the regulator it could be said to consist in increasing the value of X at each review. Not surprisingly, especially in view of the hostility demonstrated in the exchanges between British Gas and the regulator, in the early days regulatory relations were characterized as conflict games based on asymmetric information. Though some regulators and companies see this as a process of confrontation, others do not. Delaying tactics can be deployed. Indeed reviews or planned reforms of the system, such as the introduction of competition in electricity in 1998 often seem to produce a certain amount of brinkmanship on the part of the regulated companies. But Stelzer's description of a High Noon confrontation can by no means be applied to all company-regulator interactions (Coen and Willman, 1998, p. 2). For both parties there can be incentives to co-operate – which is after all in the British tradition of 'regulation by negotiation' – and relationships can even become collusive. The closed environment of the industry may give the two sides an opportunity to negotiate and reach a win-win situation. For the regulator the information asymmetry is reduced and for the company the regulatory uncertainty is lessened. The regulation initiative research programme at LBS found that significant developments have taken place within companies since privatization (Coen and Willman, 1998). To start with, companies, still monopolistic and centralised, risk-averse and not very cost conscious, merely reacted with suspicion to the regulator; few management resources were devoted to dealing with regulation and the regulator's requests for information were often viewed as illegitimate. Those who had been involved with the privatization process often took the lead, stressing the importance of impressing the City and outperforming the price review. Gradually things changed and though still somewhat perfunctory and reactive, a proper regulatory function emerged, usually led by the finance department, though no particular incentive to co-operate was yet recognised. In some cases, the regulatory affairs department was seen as almost part of the regulator's office (Scott et al., 1997). Most privatized companies now have regulatory departments whose task is to try and predict the regulator's response and generally reduce uncertainty.

Diplomacy is important since co-operation with the regulator could lead to less strict monitoring and a more understanding response to subsequent lapses; all the same, to get a good review it may be necessary to treat the regulator with some care. Much time and effort is put into trying to work out what the regulator will do. This 'gaming' activity takes up a large amount of management time, which represents a significant cost. A more strategic approach has begun to appear. Issues other than price reviews become more important; firms are increasingly political, recognising the necessity for co-ordination and mediation and for all to 'sing from the same hymn sheet' and also to use lobbying techniques. For example, Transco, advised by McKinsey, set up in 1997 a new 40-strong regulation department in an attempt to improve its relations with Ofgas, which had continued to be very confrontational, no doubt a legacy from McKinnon and Spottiswoode. The contrast between the first two gas regulators and McCarthy was striking. The complete lack of trust which had previously existed, with the regulator making impromptu public statements, was replaced by a much more open relationship, in which the issues to be resolved were clearly set out.

For a regulated company a price review will entail providing answers to the regulator's requests for information of all kinds. Some of this will be seen as impossible – these enquiries are often called 'fishing expeditions'; this process is time-consuming for staff in the company and the regulator's office. Quality of staff can be a key determinant of the outcome, as can the standard of organization. A review consists of consultations, which are public, and investigations, which are not. Consultations cover planning and network performance, how charges are fixed, and customer service. Investigations cover past and future capital investment programmes, especially the replacement of assets, future revenue predictions and operating expenditure and how these would be financed. It would also, for example, cover comparisons between RECs. All this data is analysed to see what scope there is for efficiency savings. The conclusion is likely to be an increased value for X, but could well include in addition specific targets on quality, such as services for the disabled, dealing with customers who have difficulty paying or improvement in advice services.

The review process tends to be characterized by a 'meetings culture'. This was especially true of the 1995 OFTEL review, when they took place constantly, within the office and with BT as well as wider consultations. Even though there was a certain degree of consensus, on the information, and also to a degree on the outcome, information from the company was not always forthcoming, with the excuse familiar to all regulators, that it was not available in the form requested. It was at this time that Iain Vallance described OFTEL as creating 'a hostile and unpredictable regulatory environment' (Lapsley and Kilpatrick, 1997, p. 81) even though BT had accepted virtually all OFTEL's reviews. Instead of using its power to insist on the information, OFTEL acquired it by other means, including from the other telephone companies (Hall et al., 2000, p. 137).

Though described as a 'ritual dance' (*Times,* 19 Nov. 1998) with the regulators, negotiations, for that is what they are, though Clare Spottiswoode never recognised them as such, can go right to the wire. In the closing stages of the 1999 water review, the regulator moderated his expectations of the savings the companies could make and cut the average price reduction to 12 per cent. There were two reasons for this; one was that the government made a last minute move to increase the budget for environmental spending and the other was that the companies produced new information (*Times,* 26 Nov. 1999).

The 1999 electricity distribution price review by Ofgem initially called for one-off (otherwise known as P-nought or P0) price cuts of between 12 and 37 per cent. Protests from Northern and Midlands that 10 per cent of jobs might have to go, were said to be viewed by the regulator as scaremongering (*Utility Week,* 15 Oct. 1999). All the same, the regulator reduced most of them, allowing extra money for improving customer services and saying that the most efficient companies should earn a higher rate of return. Similarly the 1999 periodic review of water prices brought forth complaints that employment would have to fall by as much as 25 per cent and allegations that as a result the companies would not be able to fulfil their statutory obligations. Job cuts were announced immediately after the final determination was published, but many had already been planned. From the point of view of the regulator there was a feeling that if none of the companies wanted to take the matter to the Competition Commission, perhaps the review had been too lenient. In the event, Mid Kent and Sutton and East Surrey decided to do so.

The regulator needs information of all kinds, operational statistics as well as accounting information, but there are powerful forces working against this. It is often in the interests of the companies not to disclose information or even not to collect it, especially on costs, since if a company is producing more efficiently than its competitors, the regulator may alter his approach to the whole industry (Littlechild, 1996). Or it may release commercially valuable information that could be of advantage to another producer.

The 1999 water review was notable for the wide range of consultation and discussion with every possible interested party. These included many in the financial sector such as pension fund managers, banks, analysts as well as consumer bodies and other regulators. In spite of this and the immense amount of paper generated, the water companies themselves did not clearly understand how the prices were arrived at, especially since they may be burdened with extra obligations. They also disagreed with Byatt on capital costs. More unusually he had removed the windfall tax on dividends from the balance sheets, so that they do not fall on the consumer (Mayer, 1999).

Reluctance to disclose information on the grounds of commercial confidentiality has been widespread even where a monopoly is involved. An Ofgas submission to the MMC about Transco pricing had gaps where figures should have been, and two consultants' reports for the same enquiry were also kept secret (CA, 1997, p. 311). Water companies show a similar secretiveness. Embryonic competition at the boundaries of water regions (known as inset appointments) was long delayed by the failure of those involved to share information with each other (Ofwat press release 25 Nov. 1997). This is understandable. The information will reach several different audiences. Letting competitors and potential entrants know that a company has low costs might be in its interest as it could deter entry, but the regulator might seek to impose a tighter price cap. Why spend valuable time collecting information that might be used against you? Apart from failing to produce statistics, or producing them at the last minute it is possible to produce too much or irrelevant or opaque information. Helpful information is up to date, accurate and consistently presented. The companies are unlikely to give the regulator the information he wants presented in the most useful and consistent manner unless some pressure is put on them to do so. It is worth noting, however, that greater transparency and the need for more information may be useful, but does not always work in the interest of the regulator and the consumer. For instance, the publication of price schedules can lead to collusion that in turn may give rise to anti-competitive behaviour (Waddams Price, 1997a, p. 196).

Accounting separation

The privatization legislation provided for separate accounting for core and peripheral businesses; the RECs for instance were ordered to keep separate accounts for distribution and supply businesses. But the two national organizations, BT and BG were still left with huge core businesses within which cross subsidies and price discrimination could take place. Allocation of costs has to be done to deal with this; the Activity Based Costing (ABC) technique was gradually introduced, with Ofwat as usual leading the way (Burns, 1995a, p. 18). The RECs have not been required to produce such detailed information, but even the water companies still have a certain amount of discretion on how they present the information and they can use different methodologies for depreciation.

Separate accounting for regulated and unregulated business and core and peripheral activities should improve the information available to regulators. The theoretical basis for the idea of comparative or yardstick competition is that it can overcome the information problem for regulators in an industry such as water and electricity distribution where competition is unlikely because of the network characteristics. The information provided by the comparators should enable the regulator to compare the activities of similar monopolies across the country. In practice, this remains unsatisfactory at least in electricity, since the variations in size of network, density of population and type of load are so great between the different RECs. The amount of information required to make the comparisons would be so difficult and costly to collect and the regulation so intrusive that it would constitute a reversal of the decision to have a simple price control mechanism (Weyman-Jones, 1995, p. 441).

The information problem presents itself in various different ways. In the electricity industry, during the post-privatization phase, the information asymmetry was increased by the existence of the 'golden shares'[7] held by the government in each of the twelve RECs. Since they were immune from takeover, the information on their costs, revenues, and investment plans and so on did not come into the public domain. According to Newbery 'the supply of statistical information' dried up (TIC, Session 1994–5, HC 481-II, p. 92). It was accounting information in particular that was in short supply in all the utilities after privatization, since costings appropriate for nationalized industries would not transfer well to private companies. Accountants were not much in evidence at OFTEL when it was first set up, so Carsberg used the economists who were available. Both for RPI − X and for the interconnection issue which was vital for the introduction of competition, their work was based on modelling, using information from Mercury, from the Hull telephone company, from the cable companies and from overseas. After 'distilling' all their answers a report was then presented to BT for comment. This proved a good substitute for a detailed costing exercise (Carsberg, 1994, p. 8).

Nowadays, sophisticated and large-scale costing exercises are done, using activity based costing. Transco conducted one such exercise in 1994, which resulted in a much deeper understanding by the company of its costs, but Ofgas cut the standing charge which emerged from this exercise from £26 to £15. And, though the company published a great deal of information in connection with the project, they drew the line at publishing the cost drivers; 'there comes a point where under intensive regulation the managerial responsibility to improve the business should have some advantage at least in terms of understanding of the business' (Copley, 1994, pp. 77–8).

But the key to transparency and hence accountability is accounting information. Here complications proliferate. Unlike the US, the UK has no specific utility accounting standards. Since accountants and economists take different views of profits and other figures, the former tending to look backwards and the latter forwards, there has been a good deal of confusion about the provision of information for price reviews. It was not till late 1998 that OFFER issued a consultation paper to the RECs on this topic. Accounts can be prepared on different bases, the key distinction being that between historic cost accounting (HCA) and current cost accounting (CCA).

After the privatization programme had got under way, a Whitehall committee chaired by Ian Byatt did develop methods of accounting to measure economic costs, especially the cost of capital. CCA accounting was the chosen approach. Analysts and investors however prefer historic cost accounting, which is the traditional form. It records assets in the balance sheet at their historic purchase cost, even though the market value may have altered. CCA is based on current replacement cost. Though each may provide useful information they will show quite different profit pictures (Vass, 1999a, p. 237). HCA, since it is based on outdated information and asset values, does have serious weaknesses. Regulators prefer CCA figures partly because the use of HCA works against potential entrants. Industry sees CCA as too subjective, but the regulator can more easily detect cross-subsidy, price discrimination and other regulatory offences (Foster, 1992, p. 250). Cost allocation becomes more significant as competition advances and has become more of a feature of MMC–Competition Commission enquiries, for example the investigation into mobile telephone charges. But it is not a simple process and allocating common costs can be expensive and especially problematic where the company has unregulated as well as regulated activities (*Utilities Journal*, May 1999).

The MMC has contributed much to improving consistency across the industries which has helped to achieve a more stable long term cost of capital (Morris, 1996). Autumn 1999 brought the announcement of a regular meeting five times a year between the directors of Ofgem, OFTEL, OFREG, Ofwat and the rail regulator. Such meetings were not a completely new departure; they had happened on a less frequent basis for some years (NAO, 1996), but it represents an advance if they can co-operate on technical issues. This acknowledges the growth of multi-utilities and the topics to be dealt with included cost of capital, regulatory accounting an important additional source of information, and competitive markets (*Utility Week*, 15 Oct. 1999). David Edmonds of OFTEL meets the OFT and Independent Television Commission every six weeks.

The diversification and merger activity that has taken place in the utility sector since privatization also has an important impact on availability of information. If a company becomes a subsidiary, separate reports and accounts are no longer required; if the takeover was by a foreign company, this situation is exacerbated since different accounting conventions make analysis more difficult. Several proposed mergers in the water industry have been blocked; for instance those in 1996 by both Wessex Water and Severn Trent, and comparators have been largely maintained. This was not the case in electricity. The regulator or Secretary of State can insist on licence modifications to protect consumers in situations such as when United Utilities was formed in 1995 and Hyder in 1996. Competitive tendering within these diversified or merged companies is not often carried out as it should be, so cost allocation is virtually impossible. In the absence of any policy guidance from the Secretary of State, the electricity and water regulators developed their own, insisting on amendments to licences, ensuring access to information and customer protection, but attempts at separate listing were not successful. The enduring problem of the information asymmetry was thrown into sharp relief by the first attempted takeover of a REC in late 1994.

The re-opening of the RECs' distribution review, 1995

In March 1995 the electricity regulator surprised companies, consumers and the City alike when he announced that the prices and the figure for X set for the distribution businesses of the regional electricity companies would be re-considered. This episode more than any other in the mid-1990s brought into question the system of utility regulation established a decade earlier. It also served to demonstrate the gulf between City thinking and consumer attitudes.

The prices set in August 1994 had been due to be in force from April 1995 till 1999, that is after the introduction of competition into the domestic electricity market which was planned for 1998. Littlechild had considered setting prices just until 1998 but had rejected the idea since to do so might foster an undesirable level of instability and uncertainty (Prosser, 1997, p. 163). The new levels for distribution charges, which account for about 25 per cent of the average electricity bill, were cut by amounts ranging from 11 to 17 per cent, to take effect from April 1995. The figure for X was -2. The new charges implied a reduction of £12 to £16 on an average annual bill, which would be offset by the impending increase of VAT on domestic fuel from 8 to 17.5 per cent.

Earlier in the year the expectation had been for a much harsher review, involving price cuts of up to 30 per cent and an X of -4 (*Times*, 12 Aug. 1994). The announcement of a relatively lenient regime for 1995–9 only served therefore to fuel further rises in the RECs' shares that had been outperforming the market all summer. The reaction from consumers' organizations was that price cuts should have been larger; some in the City suggested that the wool had been pulled over the regulator's eyes. The fact that the water regulator had just completed a generous review may have intensified the reaction.

All the English and Welsh RECs accepted this settlement, but Scottish Hydro, a vertically integrated company with special geographical problems, decided to appeal to the MMC. This was the first occasion on which the Commission had had the opportunity to investigate any part of the ESI.

The 'golden shares' held by the government in each of the RECs were due to expire in March 1995 after which time takeovers or mergers would be permissible. The RECs had been sold off in unsettled markets when the Gulf War was about to break out. More than any other such sale the prices achieved had been lower than they need have been. Unlike transmission and supply, the distribution prices had a positive value for X in most cases, so this review was likely to have greater impact. Interest in these companies was clearly increasing long before the expiry date, much of it emanating from the US. They were local monopolies, carrying very little debt and no major new investment was required. In short, they were 'low risk cash cows ripe for takeover' (Newbery in TIC, Session 1994–5, HC 481-II, p. 92).

It was a British company, however, Trafalgar House, that opened the bidding at the end of 1994 when it launched a hostile takeover for Newcastle-based Northern Electric. The company mounted a vigorous defence, which included more than £500 million in inducements to its shareholders to remain loyal. It promised big cuts in costs, special payments to shareholders of £5 per share, for shares that had been sold for only £2.40 in 1990. It announced plans to increase gearing and raise dividends (Robinson, 1996, p. 132), thus revealing to the regulator that their costs were lower than they had previously claimed. The battle continued until early March when Littlechild made his surprise statement. It came the day after the unsold portion of shares in National Power and PowerGen had been put on the market, making instant profits for those who invested. He was 'minded', he said, to reconsider the charges he had set. RECs shares fell by 10 to 15 per cent, shares in the generators rather less and there was also anxiety about whether the flotation of the NGC planned for the end of the year would go ahead. In the ensuing round of recriminations it became clear that Littlechild had warned the government that he was thinking of making an announcement on the matter and twice changed his mind about whether or not to go ahead (*Times*, 28 July 1995). Lawyers and bankers had been consulted and it had been decided that the new flotation should proceed.

This was not the first time that Littlechild had been the subject of criticism. In 1992 when there was a political crisis over the coal industry, a series of events described in detail in Chapter 5, he had been criticized by the Trade and Industry Committee over his reluctance to investigate the purchasing policies of the RECs. Even more to the point he had been asked by the Energy Committee to bring forward the distribution review since the electricity companies were making such high profits (Energy Committee, Session 1991–2, HC 113, para. 92). At that time he had rather sententiously announced,

> 'If a regulator is seen to intervene constantly in the operations of a company, there will be an adverse effect on the incentive to that company to improve its efficiency and reduce costs. The degree of regulatory risk to which it is subjected may be perceived as greater. There may be consequently some increase in the rate of return which investors require and so a higher level of prices to customers in the long run.'
>
> (OFFER, press release, 9 June 1992)

He had also acknowledged in the OFFER annual report the pressure to bring forward the review, but would not yield to it, using the same arguments and much the same words: 'it would introduce additional uncertainty about regulation' (OFFER Annual Report 1992, p. 6). Even in August 1994, the very month he got it wrong, he had expounded the virtues of stability. 'Frequent adjustment of price controls invites interference in the day to day operation of companies. This would create the very confusion and inefficiency which privatization and arm's length regulation were designed to reduce' (quoted Prosser, 1997, p. 163). Thus Littlechild was wholeheartedly defending the system he had created.

The utility sector, continuously controversial in the 1990s, was by March 1995 in worse odour than ever. The question of directors' salary increases and share options was now added to other longer running debates. This change of heart by the architect of the system thus became a matter of acute public interest.

The reason given was that the bid for Northern had revealed the enormous amounts of cash held by the company and presumably the other companies as well. But additionally there were the rising share prices and requests from parliamentary committees and the consumer groups such as the CA and the NCC and even the ECCCG. This added up to a great deal of pressure. On 24 March 1995 Littlechild confirmed that he would redo the review. In early July, it was revealed that the charges set for April 1995 to April 1996 would stand, but that from April 1996, new controls would come into force. These were further one-off cuts of up to 13 per cent and a tougher X of -3. One cynical commentator expressed the view that the director had worked backwards from the price controls he thought appropriate (TIC, Session 1996–7, HC 50-II, p. 138).

The MMC's report on Scottish Hydro had appeared shortly before; it took the view that the regulator had placed too high a value on the company's assets, and that redundancy payments should be absorbed not added on. Following a similar procedure, and allowing a rate of return of 7 per cent, Littlechild came up with his new figures (MacKerron and Boira Segarra, 1996, p. 106). The resolution was therefore largely an accounting one and since he was following the MMC, the likelihood of any appeals was very slender. The whole episode, however, showed up the shortcomings of his review procedures. The inadequacy of information was serious; why was he not aware of the true financial picture in the summer of 1994? There was at that time no standardization of accounting methods among the RECs and the work had been done in haste. The franchise drop[8] in April had been described as chaotic (TIC, Session 1994–5, HC 481, p. 86). Perhaps it was the case that Littlechild's commitment to competition was such that he did not press the companies for more information and disseminate more himself, to avoid the possibility of firms co-ordinating their strategies. Certainly it is hard to disagree with those who argued that the events of 1994–5 in the ESI proved that competition is indeed a revelatory mechanism. 'Even where there is no rivalry in the product market, the market for corporate control helps fill the regulator's information gap' (Robinson, 1996, p. 133).

On regulatory risk, a major preoccupation of the City and those who had bid up the price of Northern, Littlechild was also open to criticism; but such risk is inherent in the system, and it could not be argued that the RECs were losers. Littlechild told the Public Accounts Committee (PAC, Session 1996–7, HC 89, para. 47) that for a regulator to claw back profits retrospectively would be a breach of faith with investors; and would increase perceptions of regulatory risk. Though difficult to untangle, it must therefore be assumed that he was looking forward and trying to set a reasonable rate for the next few years. But it was the beginning of a learning process for both regulators and investors. In spite of the setbacks of March, share prices recovered well.

The Trafalgar House bid for Northern was finally withdrawn in August 1995, but during the late summer and autumn there was a series of similar bids for other RECs and by the following spring only four out of the 12 RECs remained independent. Though Littlechild was accused of having fatally undermined the principle of RPI − X regulation, and there were calls for his resignation which he firmly resisted, the formula continued to be used, albeit with a generous seasoning of rate of return. The regulator himself continued in office for another four and a half years, thus establishing a modicum of independence for the species, if not confirming its popularity. The parliamentary committee, which had previously criticized him so severely, vindicated his actions (TIC, Session 1994–5, HC 481, para. 94) and greater benefits were delivered to consumers. But change was on the way; the Labour party had committed itself to a windfall tax and the wide discretion of regulators was to be limited, possibly by the introduction of boards and closer government guidelines. This episode undoubtedly contributed to the increasing pressure for reform.

3
A Fair Deal for Consumers?

'Universal service is about making sure that what most of us take for granted is available to everyone.'*

At the time of privatization, the main objective was a successful sale. Propaganda aside, consumer concerns were not a high priority in the legislation which established the new regulatory regimes, even though the starting point was ostensibly the protection of consumers large and small against monopoly power. Over the years however, this has undergone a fundamental change and the Utilities Act 2000 made consumer protection a primary duty for the energy regulator, though similar provisions for telecommunications were withdrawn.

The first few years after privatization had brought some benefits in terms of lower prices for gas, electricity and telecoms, but there were problems with quality, some of them serious. In addition, high salaries for directors and generous dividends for shareholders plus several badly handled episodes involving poor quality of service created widespread resentment and the utilities became very unpopular. The discontent which had been generated was put to good use by the Labour party when it devised and promoted the windfall tax in the run up to the 1997 general election. The abandonment of Clause Four of the Labour party constitution made it easier for the opposition to adopt a pro-consumer stance, and like the Conservatives before them they gradually came around to accepting with reservations the reforms of their predecessors, including the introduction of competition into the gas and electricity markets. The likely impact of this reform, especially on lower income groups was a matter of debate among consumer groups

*Oftel, 1999, p. 4.

as well as politicians. The distributional implications of competition were not addressed before the 1997 election but were subsequently to become an important focus for the party (Currie, 1997, p. 7). The party's approach to the utilities was founded on the idea of improving the lot of the consumer, in particular the less advantaged consumer. One strand of the new government's social policy was to tackle social exclusion, a significant component of which was to make utility services available to all at affordable prices.

The regulators' duties

Access, equity and distributional aspects are of relatively small concern in a commercial world. But the essential nature of these goods is such that what Ernst calls the 'random stewardship of the free market' (Ernst, 1994, p. 53) was judged inadequate to ensure access for all. For this reason the regulators were given social obligations and the Utilities Act 2000 makes these stronger and more explicit. The existence of the social obligations confirms the special nature of the utilities; RPI − X price capping may have delivered price cuts for some services but there remains a debate about fairness and distribution of any benefits. A social obligation is an obligation to supply in a case where on a strictly economic basis it would not be done. The regulators have to ensure that reasonable demands are met, though the precise definition of this varies. In the gas industry, this applies to all suppliers, not just BG; in telecoms it applies to BT alone because of its 'ubiquity'. The duties of the regulators also include taking special account of those who are disabled or of pensionable age or in the case of gas, chronically sick as well. This covers things like a register of disabled customers, a password system, aids and adaptations and help with bill reading. Braille bills are also available. The water and electricity regulators also have to protect the interests of those in rural areas. This is what the legislation says, but the implications are far from clear; and there is no doubt that there is a potential conflict with the duty to encourage competition. The consensus among companies and regulators is that these obligations are political in character; indeed it can be argued that they – companies and regulators – effectively create social policy when they take decisions which affect access to these services. Meeting these obligations is a condition of getting and keeping a licence; but they must at the same time avoid undue discrimination in favour of particular groups.

Regulators themselves have not always agreed on the precise nature of their role with respect to the consumer and interpretations have varied over time and from one regulator to another. McKinnon, the feisty first gas regulator placed himself firmly in the consumer's corner and fought hard against British Gas. OFTEL, too, under its various Directors General (DGs) could be seen in general to be on the side of the consumer. In spite of this in the first five to ten years after privatization it was not apparent that the consumer's lot was improving in terms of lower prices or better standards of service. When Clare Spottiswoode replaced McKinnon in 1993 she continued his fight. Indeed, she made a public declaration that her role was that of a defender of the consumer. Ian Byatt, the water regulator, could not agree with this; indeed perhaps reflecting his long experience as a Whitehall civil servant, he said it would be illegal. Intervention on prices became quite frequent all the same, with periodic reviews being brought forward in 1992 and 1997. Stephen Littlechild the electricity regulator did not intervene a great deal to protect consumers, but this was consistent with his general approach.

The legislation on telecoms, though arguably less essential to life than the other services under discussion and certainly seen as much closer to a commodity than a utility – though definitions here are not very clear – gives the regulator social obligations as primary duties. These include emergency services, public call boxes, 192 calls and services in rural areas. BT also provides a 'no frills' service aimed at poorer customers, which allows incoming calls and 999 calls, with few other outgoing calls. The costs of these services are geographically averaged. In a rational market remote places would not be supplied at the same price. An extreme example of this is a hotel in a remote Welsh valley that wanted fifteen lines installed: the cost of this was so high that it would have been cheaper for BT to buy the hotel and close it down (Ash, 1993, p. 37). Successive regulators have increased social obligations on BT. This process, described by Yarrow as 'regulatory opportunism' (Yarrow, 1996, p. 70), is criticised by those who favour less regulation and more competition, but has an obvious attraction for politicians who can gain kudos for such benefits handed to specific groups of consumers, especially if the cost is not transparent.

Historical cross subsidies

Social obligations are far from being a novel idea; they were part and parcel of the new regime when nationalization took place in the 1940s. The services they provided were perceived as 'merit goods' (Helm, 1997, p. 9). Costs were mostly averaged across customers. Gas prices (post-1972) were traditionally uniform across the country, like telephone and postal charges, though until the 1980s they had varying standing charges, while water and electricity varied, depending on the regional supplier, but were still averaged out within each region. Standing charges were normally below cost, with the differential recovered by higher running rates as Waddams Price and Hancock have shown (1998). So prices did not necessarily reflect costs, which inevitably varied according to geographical location, peak demand and payment method.

Rural areas, not surprisingly, cost more to supply than urban ones; and distance from the source of supply also increases costs. Since most gas is landed in the north east of the UK, gas in the south west costs far more to supply than in other areas. To a certain extent this is also true of electricity, because more is generated in the north and more consumed in the south, and there are transmission losses, too. Costs can also vary at different times, depending on levels of demand. Telephone calls are subject to different charges, depending on the time of day and day of the week. Electricity is cheaper at night on a special tariff. Such precise charging methods are not worthwhile for gas and water for residential consumers, for technical reasons. Those who consume small amounts are also more expensive to supply, or to put it another way, less profitable. These are likely to be the less well off households. Bad payers are also expensive. Up to 30 per cent are slow, do not pay or become debt problems and they can cost ten times more than prompt payers do (CA, 1997, p. 116).

Lower income groups have particular problems, which will be looked at later in this chapter. Many issues, however, concern all consumers.

Price and quality

In spite of negative public perceptions of privatization, the fact is that consumers now pay less in real terms for their gas, electricity and telephone than they did in the past. Domestic bills, however, have not fallen by nearly as much as industrial ones, which have seen cuts of up to 50 per cent across the utilities. Average household electricity bills (quarterly credit, including VAT where charged) fell from £245 in 1990, rose to £300 in 1995 and then fell to £267 in 1998. The same quarterly credit bill for an average customer in gas was £285 in 1990, £327 in 1995 and £315 in 1998. Direct debit payers paid significantly less and pre-payment meter users more. A telephone estimate is more difficult to arrive at, but there has been an average fall of about 16 per cent while line rental charges have gone up. Water on the other hand has become much more expensive; the average household bill has risen by about 40 per cent since privatization and the same is true of sewerage charges.

Lower prices are partly the result of falling oil prices and more advanced technology but also of the RPI − X formula which has forced companies to cut their costs – often by shedding labour and incidentally shunting the problem off onto the Treasury, which has to foot the bill for unemployment and other benefits. But obviously there is a close link between price and quality, and costs can also be cut by reducing the quality of the product. 'Quality degradation is a means of loosening the price cap' (Cave, 1993, p. 47), or to put it another way, 'reduced service standards are an effective price increase' (PAC 1996–7, HC 89, para. 65). And especially in the utilities quality just as obviously has a safety dimension.

Among their other functions the DGs are charged with 'setting or overseeing quality of service standards', ensuring compensation when these are not met and the monitoring of compliance by suppliers. Improving quality in all its dimensions has been an important part of their activities. Under the old regime when these industries were nationalized quality of service was not really an issue; there was no real means of judging quality and no framework for measuring it (Graham, 1993, p. 83). And in the early years, as the BT 'Quality Crisis' demonstrated, things often got worse rather than better. Privatization of BT in 1986 had been swiftly followed by a sharp deterioration in service. A number of factors were responsible, including poor industrial relations, staff cuts and the introduction of new technology and rising demand for telephones. For a while BT was portrayed as 'the most loathed institution in the country – a by-word for inefficiency' (Pitt, 1994, p. 72). As a direct result of the experience with British Gas and BT, tighter regulation of quality was incorporated in the legislation for electricity and water.

The National Consumer Council, set up in 1975, had gradually convinced public opinion that consumerism was relevant to the public services. Then in 1991 came the Citizen's Charter, an inspiration of the prime minister John Major. Its principles conformed to those of consumerism as set out by the NCC: Access, Choice, Information, Redress and Representation. The position of the apostrophe makes it clear that the citizen in question is an individual (Evans, 1993, p. 4). Consumers of gas, electricity and water had at this point no choice of supplier though there was some competition in telephones. They were being encouraged to perceive a market where none existed.

The Competition and Service (Utilities) Act of 1992 was a direct result of the Citizen's Charter, bringing all regulators' powers up to equal the last one established, OFFER. Each regulator now had the power to put in place standards that were guaranteed. Consumers were to be consulted and accountability improved. The standards were to be 'challenging but achievable', meeting the Goldilocks criterion, that is not too high and not too low but just right. There was also to be payment of compensation when they were not met.

Service standards

Standard setting, however, has its pitfalls. First, it is easy to end up with a set of standards that seem relevant but do not relate to what the customers actually want. Secondly 'as with all performance indicators there will be a tendency for the measurable to drive out the unmeasurable' (Cave, 1993, p. 57). Four main aspects can be distinguished: product quality, reliability of supply, customer interface, that is appointments and billing, and environmental problems. All have to be tackled, but the last is far more long term and likely to be far more expensive to deal with and often more difficult for consumers to judge. The case by case approach of dealing with complaints may be important for the first three, but when it comes to 'macro' aspects of quality such as EU directives on bathing beaches, a collective choice has to be made and this must be the responsibility of the regulator (Vass, 1993, p. 62). The customer cannot make an individual choice on this, cannot at least at present, choose to have a lower quality of product or service and pay less as they can when buying food, clothes or holidays. In other words consumerism is not enough.

This applies perhaps especially to water and is the reason that Ian Byatt put so much emphasis on consultation about willingness to pay for improvements such as water quality. Marginal improvements to already high standards are expensive. Unfortunately, consultation is not especially successful in that it is not easy to get meaningful answers from consumers. Ofwat's consultation on the Cost of Quality elicited only 112 responses, 73 of which were from individuals and one water company got only 17 responses from its 500,000 customers (Gardner, 1995, p. 3). The chairman of the Ofwat National Consumers Council (ONCC) admitted that this paucity of response, not only from the general public but also from local authorities, must be put down to the fact that people are not very interested, at least until a problem arises.

Spurred on by the prospect of competition in the domestic market, the companies have been trying hard over the last few years to improve their customer orientation and brand identity. Powergen has sponsored the television weather forecast, and the Eastern group supported the National Youth Theatre with a grant of nearly £900,000 (*Times*, 27 Oct. 1997), which provided a photo opportunity for Romeo and Juliet at a power station. Another company is sponsoring the Youth Hostels Association. The water industry has become keen to identify itself with conservation: Water UK and Biffa (a subsidiary of Severn Trent) are financing measures to preserve otters and their habitats (*Times*, 8 June 1998). The introduction of competition to the gas industry has resulted in increasing numbers of 'affinity deals,' marketing partnerships which are also intended to improve brand recognition and provide incentives to choose one company rather than another. Scottish Hydro teamed up with Amerada Hess, Scottish Power with the Automobile Association. The Goldfish credit card established by BG gained the participation of Boots and Asda though it also led to lengthy investigations by the Data Protection Registrar on the question of what use BG might be allowed to make of its customer information. After an initial ban, it was decided on appeal that the gas company could use data on customers gathered before privatization for the purpose of selling them products other than gas (*Utility Week*, 3 April 1998).

An obvious starting point in measuring whether or not customers are satisfied with the standard of service they receive is the level of complaints. But a rise might only reflect greater public awareness of the consumer body due to media attention. British Gas and the water companies both registered increasing levels of complaints after privatization. Charges and billing accounted for most complaints. Electricity on the other hand exhibited a marked improvement over the few years after privatization, with complaints falling steadily in most regions. An immediate introduction of customer service standards and quality checks no doubt played a big part in this, but there were also guaranteed compensation payments for failures.

In addition to the numbers of complaints, there are other standards, which can be applied across the various industries. These are probably most fully developed in the water industry and can include measures such as keeping appointments, dealing with account queries or payment arrangements, installation of meters, responding to complaints, restoring supply, giving notice of interruption. League tables can then be used to shame companies into improving their performance. A belief in the perfectibility of these organizations is part of the Ofwat philosophy and its hallmark is the search for continuous improvement. Its level of service indicators include the availability of water – though not water quality which is the responsibility of the Drinking Water Inspectorate – water pressure, loss of supply, hose pipe bans and responses to enquiries and complaints. So far, so simple: but the precise definitions are extremely technical and do not always hit the required target. For instance, on complaints, speed of response is measured, but not the level of customer satisfaction, which would be hard to do (Ogden, 1997, p. 542). Supplementary measures have been added, on meter reading and ease of telephone access, which are equally open to quibbles. An elaborate 'technology of calculation' has been constructed by which companies can be compared.

These figures can be put to several uses. They are drawn up for the Periodic Reviews and thus gain more definitive status as business objectives (and incidentally as a guideline for managers' bonuses). They are also of interest to the City both for the assessment of regulatory risk and for judgement on whether a company is spending appropriately (i.e. not too much) on customer services. But good customer relations are an asset in the important relationship with the regulator: 'one of our objectives is to be at the bottom of his hit list' said one senior manager (Ogden, 1997, p. 547).

The 'triumph of managerialism over bureaucracy' does not end there, however, for in order to ensure that the information gathered on the levels of service indicators is 'robust', another layer of management consultants has been added. Ofwat has also gone as far as comparing the performance of water companies with other sectors, not just electricity and gas but banking and insurance on response speed for bill queries. Ofgas standards included the commitment to reply to correspondence in five days; but how relevant is this when most customers make contact by telephone?

Compensation

Redress is one of the principles of the Citizen's charter. Failure to meet standards is now compensated. The superior performance of the electricity industry is doubtless due to the fact that the relatively generous payments to customers who have been let down provide a strong incentive to the companies to adhere to the standards. The £50 payouts for some electricity failures is five times greater than water companies may offer for failures in supply and 'boil water' notices. It is very hard to get compensation for low water pressure or failure of supply, and it has even proved hard to obtain for poor water quality. A parasitic infestation, cryptosporidium, has appeared in a number of areas of England and Wales over the last few years; customers have to boil water, but compensation is not automatic in such cases. The Director General decided this was inappropriate because 'boil water' notices are often used as a precautionary measure and companies, if obliged to compensate, might not introduce such notices and thus endanger public health (CA, 1997, p. 150). Individual companies have, however, introduced their own voluntary compensation schemes, some more generous than others.

These standards treat all customers the same even though they may have different preferences and once again there may be conflicting interests. 'Consumerist' approaches tend to focus on procedural matters such as keeping appointments rather than price, or payment method. The vulnerable customers want cheaper prices and easier payment methods, in other words, affordability and access. They may be more interested in how debt is handled and avoiding disconnection than service standards or mechanisms for consumer representation.

There have been, however, several much more serious episodes, when standards have been very gravely compromised. The Yorkshire Water crisis of 1995 is a case in point.

The Yorkshire Water crisis of 1995

The vital importance of water to the consumer was demonstrated during 1995, as were the difficulties for the privatized companies of dealing with consumer problems. The summer of 1995 was unusually dry and hot. July saw only half the normal amount of rainfall. Much of the country was subject to hose pipe bans, but the drought led to a full-scale crisis only in the Yorkshire Water area. An analysis of the episode demonstrates that the crisis could have been avoided, that good PR is vital, and that issues concerning the utilities, especially water, remain politically highly charged.

By August, as the level of leakages was highlighted in the press, Yorkshire Water had applied for a drought order that would ban non-essential use such as car washes, and permit more abstraction from rivers. Two other water companies, North West and South West followed suit. Trouble was already in the air: the regulator took the opportunity to seize the moral high ground by writing to the companies criticizing their service standards and threatening to force them to cut prices. The Environment Secretary, John Gummer, joined in with advice to customers on how to wash their faces, an intervention as far-cical as that in1974 by an earlier Conservative minister who, during a miners' strike, advised the nation to clean its teeth in the dark. The crisis gave the Labour opposition an opportunity to criticize the privatization programme and high executive salaries as well as the leakage rate. The windfall tax later to be controversially introduced by the Labour government was first floated as an idea at this time.

Yorkshire Water was deeply unpopular among residents before the water shortage became a crisis and this unpopularity was exacerbated in the summer of 1995 by the announcement of a special dividend totalling £50 million for which it was later strongly criticized by the regulator (Ofwat, 1996). Though the company's financial record was good, its customer complaints record was not creditable. Yorkshire undoubtedly faced far more serious problems than other regions. The Water Services Association said it was the worst drought for 200 years but in Yorkshire where water was normally abundant, the drought was apparently the worst for 500 years. The company's declared aim was to meet demand in 49 years out of 50. Elsewhere the situation was less serious. Anglian, a low rainfall area, had pushed ahead with metering and had spent £1.7 billion on infrastructure. Thames had built the London ring main that also contributed greatly to a lessening of the problems. Hose pipe bans, standpipes in the streets combined with continued hot weather coincided with buybacks and special dividends; this created a situation in which what the *Times* called the 'fragile social contract' (18 Aug. 1995) between the water companies and the public reached breaking point. Though the drought was severe, Yorkshire Water had not only underestimated demand, but also failed to implement any measures to cut leakages and tried to disguise this by implying that the shortage was the customers' fault (Ofwat, 1996).

By the end of August, Yorkshire Water was instructing its personnel not to wear uniform, for fear of attack. That its approach left a great deal to be desired was evidenced by the story that a customer who complained about the amount of money spent on advertising received a 50 pence refund, which represented the spend per household (*Economist*, 22 July 1995). A report commissioned by Ofwat later revealed the anger of some residents of the area. They saw the company as scaremongering and abusing its monopoly. Insult was added to injury when after the regulator made a statement to the effect that the water companies should consider the possibility of compensating customers who had suffered loss of service during the drought, they replied that Byatt was 'political point scoring' (*Economist*, 26 Aug.

1995). Recognition that this had been unwise was perhaps conceded in October when the ten water companies promised to spend up to £4 billion fixing leaks. Heavy rain did nothing to solve the shortages and an emergency drought order, which would permit the company to cut supplies for up to 24 hours, was sought. This was accompanied by another PR fiasco, when the chief executive claimed not to have had a bath for three months; investigation revealed that he crossed the border into Northumbria to do so. The company was forced to desperate measures in November when a contract was signed to have up to six million gallons of water a day brought from the Kielder reservoir in Northumbria by tanker at a cost of about £1 million a day. Two hundred lorries could do 1,000 journeys a day, but the towns of Halifax and Huddersfield were still threatened with alternate days without water. The company later denied that it had had plans to evacuate one million people if reservoirs ran dry (*Economist*, 23 March 1996).

Byatt had sharply criticized Yorkshire Water and also North West and South West Water. Yorkshire, he said, had known of its reliability problems for twenty years and failed to make the necessary investment. The company embarked on a £50 million programme of installing pipes and pumping stations. It also announced compensation of £2 per week for those who had suffered cuts in supply plus £15 per fortnight and later added that they would make payments of £10 to households which had been without water for 24 hours. This seemed a laughable sum to residents who simply felt that supply should not be interrupted. But it was, astonishingly, an improvement on the current situation that did not provide for compensation for lack of supply.

Yorkshire Water was fined £40 million by the regulator but Ofwat's attempts to improve compensation for customers affected by a drop in water pressure or restrictions on use were only moderately successful; nine companies, including Yorkshire refused to sign up to his proposals (CA, 1997, p. 133). Not till the Water Summit of 1997 did the companies agree to accept a licence condition that would give £10 per day up to a maximum of the average annual household bill (Ofwat, 1997, p. 53). Three years later, the company was still trying to recover from the poor performance of 1995 and the dismal reputation it had gained for its clumsy handling of the crisis. Both the group managing director and the company had failed to forecast demand properly (it rose not fell), had failed to invest sufficiently in leakage-stopping and developing a grid. Had one existed it would have been possible to pump water from east to west Yorkshire; work to make this happen was undertaken in 1996. Byatt promised to keep his 'beady eye' on the company (*Utility*

Week, 28 June 1996), attributing the problems to management failures. This episode highlights the difficulties of combining the motives of a plc with the supply of an essential commodity. In the water industry as a whole the regulator's desire to constrain price rises conflicts with the need to meet rising demand and improve quality as well as satisfy environmental requirements.

Consumer organizations

Under nationalization, consumer bodies were weak and had little influence (Ogden, 1997, p. 535). Those established at privatization developed a much stronger role, each with its own individual structure and modus operandi. Other organizations such as the PUAF, NCC, CA and the National Association of Citizens Advice Bureaux (NACAB) have also been instrumental, through lobbying parliament, Whitehall and the regulatory offices in gaining improvements for all categories of customers.

The Gas Consumers Council (GCC) was, unlike the other bodies, independent of its regulator Ofgas, though located very close by. Perhaps because of this it had the best funding and the highest profile. As a statutory body, its members were appointed by the Secretary of State. Unlike the others it had a certain amount of in-house expertise and did research on the elderly, the disabled and on self-disconnection. The fact that its director Sue Slipman, was a well-known national figure before arriving at the GCC contributed to its newsworthiness. A national body with regional outposts, its workload increased vastly when competition started in 1996.

By contrast the consumer representation for water and electricity was on a regional basis integrated with the regulators' offices. Each water services company has a corresponding Consumer Service Committee (CSC). The chairmen of these committees are part timers who work for five to eight days a month; the other members are volunteers. The ONCC was formed in 1993 and consists of all ten chairmen of the CSCs; all chairmen and members were appointed by the water regulator Ian Byatt. Since it grew out of meetings between regulator and chairmen it was not a statutory body, but developed an active role in spite of its unofficial standing, especially in Europe and gained a modicum of independence when Byatt decided not to take part in the meetings. The majority of complaints received by Ofwat, that is those not satisfactorily resolved by the water companies, were dealt with by the CSCs.

The regional chairmen of the Electricity Consumer Committees (ECCs) were appointed by the DG after consultation with the Secretary of State. As in the water industry, they were part time and their committee members worked on a voluntary basis. There were 14 ECCs matching the boundaries of the regional electricity companies but complaints went in the first instance to Offer, so their complaints function was much smaller. The ECCCG lobbied – most notably on the re-opening of the distribution price review in 1995 – and did research on matters such as pre-payment and disconnection.

The advisory committees on telecoms were set up rather differently; one each for England, Scotland and Wales, one for small business and one for the elderly and disabled, each with its own acronym, e.g. ENACT for England and DIEL for the disabled and elderly. They advise the DG and handle a small number of complaints and are very close to Oftel, which provides their 'secretariat' – two members of the Oftel staff (CA, 1997, p. 247). In reality it is Oftel that has played the main part in consumer representation, setting up specific advisory groups on particular issues.

These sets of committees were all less influential than the gas one because, though all three handled complaints and had advocacy and policy advice roles, they could not commission research. All could call on expertise from within the regulator's office. The electricity groups were, perhaps predictably, much less open than the water one and published far less, reflecting the style of the parent regulator. All these bodies from regulator to regional committee have a very low public profile (CA, 1997, p. 251); the Consumers' Association found that fictitious bodies were as likely as real ones to be picked out by the public in a survey. The public is barely aware of them.

The precise degree of independence possessed by these organisations is a matter of debate. On the face of it the GCC had things fairly much its own way but it still worked closely with Ofgas. The other two in contrast may have had more influence on their regulator, but no real right to get involved in policy making. In addition there was the danger of capture, by the regulator or indeed the company. The regional structure may result in conflict between one area and another. This has happened in both water and electricity, as is shown below

New, more independent bodies for energy, water and telecoms, which would have the right to be consulted, were provided for in the Utilities Bill introduced into Parliament in January 2000. The withdrawal of provisions for telecoms and water meant that their organisations would continue as before. A joint consumer council for gas and electricity is to be established. The GECC, replacing the GCC and the 14 regional ECCs, is focused exclusively on consumers, though like its predecessors it speaks for all categories of consumers, including industrial and commercial as well as domestic. Its main task is to handle complaints, though the regulatory office might become involved if the necessity of a licence change arose. It is intended to be a highly visible, partisan consumer advocate, a 'trusted guide', providing more powerful consumer representation. A 'memorandum of understanding' clarifying roles and responsibilities between the new council and Ofgem aims at a better co-ordinated and less ad hoc relationship than before. There were fears in some quarters that independence might mean impotence. There were two main causes of anxiety. Companies might be able to block publication of some material, which they saw as commercially sensitive, though this would not include statistics on complaints, energy efficiency targets or standards of performance. Secondly, the regional organizations were to be severely cut back and there was to be greater reliance on peripatetic teams. The establishment of regional committees would require the approval of the Secretary of State and they might not be able to make formal links with other consumer-orientated organizations such as CABx and Trading Standards Offices.

Just how far consumer councils should push for improvements in performance of the kind discussed above, when it is what they will be judged on, is a matter for debate. Quality improvement is far from costless, however and this is an issue that was often fudged by the consumer councils (Waddams Price, 1998). They have no cost constraints. It is the company and the consumer that will foot the bill.

There is another set of questions about advocacy by consumer bodies which relates to attempts such as that to reduce costs for particular groups, for instance those who use pre-payment meters. Any reduction in charges will be paid for by all consumers including some of the very poor. Here, once again, matters of regulation merge into politics and it may legitimately be asked which section of the whole consumer population is to be represented when interests conflict. A clear example of conflict occurred in September 1999, when the DETR issued guidance on subsidy for those on low incomes whose water supply was metered. There was a very negative reaction from the ONCC, which put out a statement that it was undesirable for customers in general to subsidize those with low incomes or special needs, adding that 'the water charging system should not be used to achieve the government's social policy objectives' (ONCC press release, 11/99).

The tendency to broaden regulation in the direction of social issues is due to the public's interest in them, no doubt helped by lobby groups. Though it is widely argued by economists that these social costs should be paid from Treasury funds so as to avoid distortions in the markets for energy, water or telecoms, other groups and individuals have campaigned to extend the special protection afforded to pensioners and the disabled to low income groups of all kinds. The Trade and Industry Committee's report on Energy Regulation published in March 1997, made this a recommendation. Many witnesses told the committee that consumer protection should be given a higher priority and the committee itself took the view that it would be undesirable to rule out the regulatory system being used as a tool of government policy (TIC, Session 1996–7, HC 50, para. 145). One argument in favour of this is that the benefit system sometimes works against those on low incomes, since the RPI is based on average prices for each item included and they may be paying more; nor are regional differences, which can be substantial, reflected in benefits.

When, after the 1997 election a comprehensive review of the utilities and their regulation was announced, two changes could immediately be discerned, though signs had been detectable well beforehand. Each regulator in turn giving evidence to the review hastened to assure the DTI that they were consumer champions. Littlechild in particular seemed to have altered his view: 'the protection of customers is of paramount importance and has always been at the centre of my priorities and policies' (*Utility Week*, 17 Oct. 1997). In addition, the focus on the impact of competition on vulnerable groups intensified. The new Industry Minister John Battle expressed concern about differential pricing for pre-payment customers. He asked the regulator to investigate how they could have a better deal and Ofgas set up a pre-payment steering group in May 1997.

The Green Paper

When the results of the utilities review was finally published as a Green Paper in spring of 1998, it took the consumer viewpoint not only in the title *A Fair Deal for Consumers*, but in the whole approach. Most of the criticisms which had been levelled at the system over the years were addressed, though the ideas of sharing windfall gains with consumers and intervening on directors' pay did not long survive publication. Proposed reforms which remained on the agenda included: issuing guidance to regulators so their duties would be more clearly defined and stressing consumer needs, organizing new and better fora for customer representation, and offering more help to low income customers. It would now be policy to ensure that all customers including those on low incomes should receive the benefits of competition and the idea was floated that the distribution businesses should make differential charges to assist pre-payment customers. Just as pricing policy was not questioned under nationalization, the licences of the privatized utilities and of the regulators were unclear how far the previous pattern of cross subsidies should be continued or financed.

The Green Paper thus identified a social dimension for which the government, not the regulator should set the agenda, but it was not strong on the practicalities of helping low income groups and said nothing on how or indeed whether the tax and benefit system should be used in this context. The energy regulators were instructed to develop an action plan, but when it appeared in June 1998, it was a disappointment in that it had little to say that had not already been said. The declared aim was to ensure that the disadvantaged customers, as well as others, benefited from improved efficiency, but fairness was to be equally important: no easy task in a competitive market. The regulator therefore had to achieve a balance between efficiency and social equity. The complex issues of how to deal with the disadvantaged presented both economic and political problems.

Politicians hoped that regulators and the industries concerned would produce solutions, while they saw these as political matters probably best dealt with by the Treasury. However it soon became clear that the previous emphasis on pre-payment meter (PPM) consumers was inadequate. By the end of the year, the focus had shifted towards the concept of Fuel Poverty (DTI, 1998). This idea had been around for some time (PUAF had been set up in 1989 and campaigned on all such issues), but now gained a new currency and was set to alter the emphasis of policy.

The DETR defined as 'fuel poor' any household which was obliged to spend ten per cent or more of disposable income on fuel to achieve adequate warmth. This approach had the appeal of being open to practical solutions based on energy efficiency. The Home Energy Efficiency Scheme (HEES) set up in 1991, provided for insulation and heating improvements and was now to be extended. Targeting was relatively simple since it went to households in receipt of an income- or disability-based benefit and an enhanced scheme was available to pensioners. Wide consultations took place with organizations ranging from Age Concern to the Energy Saving Trust (DETR, 1998). Addressing fuel poverty did however have the countervailing disadvantage of being an issue that would involve many groups and government departments. The minister, John Battle, was in favour of 'joined up thinking' and this was what such an approach required, but it also carried the risk of accountability being harder to achieve.

However, the appointment in early 1999 of Callum McCarthy, a Blairite and former civil servant to replace Littlechild and Spottiswoode seemed to provide someone who was ready to accept some of the responsibility and demonstrated the energy to push the approach forward. He announced that a fresh look was needed at the problems of the disadvantaged and pointed out that fuel poverty affected seven million households and stressed that the issues raised were not susceptible to facile solutions. Nor could the regulator take responsibility for the whole effort: 'Dealing with them requires a range of responses from government as a whole' (OFFER/Ofgas press release, 8 Feb. 1999).

This was spelt out further in May 1999 in a discussion paper. 'The scale and nature of the problems call for a response from many organisations... Offer and Ofgas, the government, particularly the Department of the Environment, Transport and the Regions (DETR) and the department of Social Security, local authorities, suppliers of electricity and gas, providers of banking services to low income households, voluntary organisations and consumer representatives' (OFFER/Ofgas, 1999).

There was therefore evidence of a real political thrust behind this and much had changed in Labour's first two years. The OFFER/Ofgas merger was only one element; new consumer councils were planned and there were distinct signs of the government involving itself more closely in regulation. The Water Act, for example, had put in place powers for the Secretary of State to set charges as well as Ofwat and had outlawed disconnection. In addition the government made other moves to help the fuel poor. The 1999 budget included provision for £100 for each pensioner household for the next winter, in advance and regardless of the weather. This was raised to £150 the following year. The 1999 Labour party conference saw a pledge by the Chancellor to install central heating systems in homes of low income groups free of charge, through the 'Affordable Warmth' agreement with Transco (*Utility Week*, 8 Oct. 1999). This was put into effect in the budget of March 2000.

Debt and disconnection

This type of issue is not within the regulator's direct control; pricing issues are. Disconnection, pre-payment and fuel poverty have been highlighted in turn. They all represent aspects of the problems of poverty, but it is not easy to disentangle them. The needs of disadvantaged customers include reducing the cost of payment, widening the choice of payment methods and setting out clearer rules on disconnection.

Disconnection for debt, very common in the past, is now much rarer. Electricity companies cut off over 1,000 customers in 1994–5, but only 383 in 1997–8 (OFFER Annual Report, 1998, p. 38). It has now been virtually eradicated. Disconnections of gas by contrast continued to rise. Indeed they doubled between 1995 and 1997 partly due to the new billing system that gave rise to so many problems in 1995–6. By 1999 they had fallen to a little over 22,000. Water disconnection is now illegal. A court decision in 1998 that budget payment units broke the law was made statutory in the Water Act of 1999.

Disconnection is a contentious issue because a warrant is required to carry it out and forced entry was often used. So it is not surprising that the Consumers Association (CA) perceives the level of disconnections as a 'barometer to gauge whether the regulators are defending the interests of the most vulnerable consumers' (CA, 1997, p. 89). Disconnections may have fallen sharply but debt has not; there are many who find paying their utility bills a big problem and who spend a significant proportion of their income on heat, light and water. The licences have encouraged companies to install PPMs where there is debt. Although originally an important factor in the decision to install the meter, at any given moment most are not collecting debt. 'Smart card' technology allows the companies to recover debt and provides them with a revenue stream. For the customers it can also be a useful budgeting method but does have its drawbacks, one being the need to travel to a post office or other charging point. A more serious potential disadvantage is that possession of one of these meters can lead to self-disconnection, the effect of which is to shift the risk and the problem from the supplier to the consumer.

The less well off customers who have these meters were initially almost the exclusive focus of concerns about the disadvantaged. A PPM is a more complex piece of equipment than a standard meter, especially for gas, and therefore costs more to supply and operate. Some electricity companies that no longer disconnect will still force entry to install a PPM. They numbered more than 3 million across England and Wales in 1997 (up from 1.8 m in 1991, Offer, 1997, p. 84), compared with 1.5 million for gas. Gas generally has lower standing charges for PPM customers, though this may not be true of the new entrants. Some have zero standing charges for credit consumers, but the unit charge is usually higher; electricity has higher standing charges and sometimes higher unit costs as well. The position for BT is rather different, though a PPM is a possibility for the future; almost one million are cut off each year, many of whom are swiftly reconnected to the network.

Most gas PPM users do have access to a bank or building society account which could be used for direct debit; but find a PPM more convenient (Doble, 1999). This choice is usually freely made, though some move over from quarterly payment after getting into arrears. Technological advance will help in the development of cheaper, more robust meters. Fuel Direct (or Water Direct), which deducts payments for gas, electricity and water at source, while not strictly speaking a payment method, helps those on benefits who have debt problems and protects them against disconnection as well as costing no more and avoiding the need to travel. The scheme, long under review by the government, is organized by the Benefits Agency and the suppliers and is rather bureaucratic. Virtually all users of gas on Fuel Direct are supplied by BGT. The problem of this method is that a fixed amount is deducted from the benefit each week, so that the price signal to the consumer is turned off (Sharratt, 2000).

Anxiety about these customers is the focus of quite a lot of lobbying activity by bodies such as Public Utilities Access Forum (PUAF), Age Concern and National Consumer Council (NCC) and NACAB. They stress that a blanket approach is unlikely to be effective, and argue that a distinction needs to be made between different age groups and subgroups of social classes. Though 50 per cent of pensioners qualify as fuel poor, only one in ten chooses a pre-payment meter, but a third of single parents use this method, while half of the very poorest do not have a pre-payment meter for electricity or gas. Thus any plan to apply differential charges to reduce the burden on PPM users would not only be unfair but also artificially increase the demand for such meters (Waddams Price and Biermann, 1998). The consumer organizations press for a greater range of frequent payment options and some progress has been made, notably with the gradual spread of Paypoint, a scheme which permits frequent small payments for council tax as well as utility bills.

The Social Action Plan published by the energy regulator in March 2000 confirmed his acceptance of the multifaceted nature of the problem. Many of the causes are beyond the power of any regulator, being a result of the type of accommodation and the age and health of the occupier. New licence changes are to facilitate frequent payments and provide better service for PPM customers when problems arise, as well as energy advice and better information. Those in debt will find it easier to change supplier and thus benefit from the competitive market. New low user tariff options are also possible. The new Home Energy Efficiency Scheme started in April 2000 is targeted mostly on low-income households and will provide insulation, low energy light bulbs and high efficiency boilers.

Competition and cross-subsidies

The redistributive effect of the price framework handed down from nationalized industry to privatized company – the RPI – X price formula was simply superimposed on the existing price structures – has already been referred to. But the redistribution remained unquestioned, even implicit. The subsidization of disabled, poor or remote customers does not fit easily into the competitive market. The effect of introducing competition into these industries is to reveal and remove the hidden cross-subsidies, so that what resembled a progressive tax regime becomes much more regressive. From the point of view of an economist this may be a move in the right direction; from a political perspective things, as always, are less clear cut. As Vickers comments:

> Most of the taxes and subsidies implicit in utility prices historically are more plausibly the result of political incentives and pressures, coupled with inertia, than of rational, normative calculation
>
> (Vickers, 1997, p. 18).

Implicit taxes, as he points out, receive far less scrutiny by Parliament and are not necessarily approved of by the electorate either. The suggestion that the supply of services to these consumers should be paid for in a different way, that is through the tax and benefit system, makes the cross-subsidies much more of a political issue than they were in the past. In the past, of course, most of the matters relating to the prices of gas, electricity and water were opaque. Even if we do not have complete transparency now it is none the less much more open than in former times.

Privatization did not immediately result in changes in the long standing state of affairs in which effectively the better off, urban dwellers subsidized the worse off or those in remote places, though BT increased its line rental to the maximum permitted by Oftel and continued to do so, so that twelve years later, facing mounting competition from other telecoms companies, the line rental had risen by 7 per cent and the average cost of calls had fallen by 40 per cent (Waddams Price and Hancock, 1998). This is a good illustration of the effects of competitive pressure: the incumbent rebalances its prices within the price cap. Thus the cross subsidies implicit within the more uniform pricing system are undermined. And just as there will be some winners, most obviously the better off who live in towns, there will also be losers. From a political point of view the losers are likely to be more important than the winners, who will probably be quiescent while the losers may express their disappointment publicly (Helm and Jenkinson, 1997, p. 9), or have it voiced for them by the various consumer bodies. As J. Stiglitz has pointed out, people are far more sensitive to losses from the status quo than to gains, 'losers scream louder and invest more in blocking policy change' (Stiglitz, 1998, p. 8). An example of this is the public anger after the MMC report on Transco in summer 1997, when price reductions were passed through to direct debit and quarterly customers but not to PPM or frequent payers. Later the reduction was conceded to other groups.

Thus a major anxiety attendant on the introduction of competition was that customers who cost more to service whether for reasons of location, low use, or payment method will suffer as competing companies 'cherry pick' the customers where the margins are greatest. So the less profitable consumers may be left to the incumbent supplier, who is then bearing the burden of the social obligations described above. In gas, attempts by the incumbent to counter this developed astoundingly fast: pricing strategies based on payment method rapidly evolved. Immediately after the announcement that the government would press ahead with introducing competition to the gas industry, British Gas brought in discounts for direct debit payers.

Distributional effects can therefore be based on geography or on income. Frequent payment methods and PPMs are far more expensive to administer than either direct debit or quarterly payment. As competition developed in the south west, payment methods were the most prominent feature in the marketing campaign. The direct debit discount has increased since early 1996 when competition began and new tariffs in 1998 further widened the differentials. Similar rebalancing has occurred in electricity prices and BT has continued to increase its line rental charges as much as it can, reducing call charges where it is vulnerable to competition. In all these ways the poorer customers do less well than others and prices become more cost reflective and less uniform.

There is all the same a considerable amount of cross subsidy in the system either for historical reasons or on account of market pressures. Regulators are supposed to be preventing undue discrimination, but as Catherine Waddams has argued, their enthusiasm to pursue this particular objective varies quite a lot (Waddams Price, 1997b). New discrepancies seem to be creeping in (*Utility Week*, 30 Jan. 1998). Privatized companies for a variety of reasons have responded to the pressure to assist vulnerable groups. Anglian Water has a cheaper tariff for 25,000 large families on income support and one for half a million single householders, for which they had to fight for approval from the regulator. If accused of discrimination, they argue that water is riddled with cross-subsidies. Anglian meters one third of its customers and has been allowed to rebalance between metered and unmetered customers to recover half of the lost revenue. Some water companies including Severn Trent have set up funds to help poor customers. There is also a special tariff for Income Support customers. Water companies of course face little or no competition.

In 1998 an attempt by the electricity industry to impose a £4 charge to subsidize PPM customers, then surcharged by every electricity supplier except Scottish Hydro, was not welcomed by the ECCs; they argued that possession of a pre-payment meter did not necessarily imply poverty, rather the reverse, it could mean a second home (*Utility Week*, 20 Feb. 1998). Electricity pre-payment customers subsequently had their surcharge capped at £15; some suppliers had been charging as much as £27. Gas PPM customers had benefited from a cross subsidy but with increasing competition, Transco attempted to charge more for these meters, which are certainly more expensive to supply and maintain. They feared that new entrants with little experience of debt management in this field would want more meters installed. The removal of a pre-existing cross subsidy was allowed, and a £10 surcharge permitted (Waddams Price, 2000).

Geographical differences are also likely to increase in the drive for cost reflectiveness. Transmission losses in electricity are to be charged on a cost-reflective basis, so that south west customers will have to pay higher prices, though this will be phased in at the regulator's request after pressure from those customers. Such moves can be seen from more than one point of view, however; Yorkshire ECC decided that consumers in their area they were being overcharged and began a campaign for them to pay less. The regulators thus have a power close to taxation; in this case those living in the north east were paying for those in the south west.

The water industry provides another example of geographical inequalities affecting the south west. The region no longer receives help from central government and other areas; its population is only 1.5 million, but there are eight million visitors to the area in the summer months when demand consequently increases by 40 per cent. Devon and Cornwall have to pay for cleaning up one third of the country's beaches. Water charges are the highest in the UK – twice the amount of the cheapest – and poorer people in the region can find themselves paying 10 per cent of their income on water charges alone. Severn Trent Water, which lacks a coastline, argues that South West Water (now Pennon) is merely being forced to invest in treatment plants which is something Severn Trent have always had to do since, without a coastline, it cannot dump sewage at sea.

Whichever way these cross subsidies go, it is very difficult for regulators and consumer bodies to untangle them and estimate how cost reflective tariffs really are. Rebalancing is likely to continue as Waddams Price and Hancock have shown, and the losers are likely to be the elderly and PPM customers. For instance, opening up metering to competition should yield efficiency gains, but it could also have the effect of making customers bear a larger part of the cost of their meter, which could mean higher PPM tariffs. The ban on water disconnection means more rebalancing to recover the lost revenue, by charging other customers more. There is thus a constant conflict between efficiency and fairness. The regulator's new duty to 'take into account the needs of those on low incomes' may mean that he, however reluctantly, may be called upon to make sure cross subsidies are used to limit the disadvantage to the poorest.

Introducing competition

The south west of England was chosen for the pilot scheme for competition in gas on the recommendation of the select committee because, due to its remoteness from gas fields and its relatively large number of poorer customers, it was an area where cost reflective transport charges were likely to have a significant negative impact. In addition there were numerous marginal parliamentary seats, where Liberal Democrats would challenge strongly at the approaching general election. The Conservatives expected to lose seats anyway and it was remote from Westminster. Half a million people in Devon and Cornwall were able to choose their gas supplier from April 1996; competition then 'rolled out' to the rest of the country by May 1998.

The initial impact was probably less marked than had been expected. For most, switching, though not hard to do, was just 'too much hassle' (TIC, Session 1994–5, HC 481, Memoranda, p. 55). However about a quarter of customers did choose another supplier and this figure was mirrored in other areas. Switching was technically easy, unlike in telecoms, which till 1997 did not provide number portability, a major barrier to entry. But problems of various sorts did arise – in final bills from British Gas, failure by entrants to get meters read at the appropriate time and in aggressive and dubious marketing tactics. Doorstep selling, something to which a third of consumers were exposed, gave rise to some anxiety when a few companies persuaded people to sign a contract under the impression that they were merely requesting more information. But the regulator decided that this method was useful and welcomed by customers (*Utility Week*, 3 April 1998). The publication of dates well in advance meant that some companies started marketing before they had their licences. In the south west, the US-owned SWEB in particular was criticized and there was an intervention by the OFT. As the Public Electricity Supplier (PES), SWEB was literally a household name and had information on all potential customers – an asset beyond price. But it withdrew from the market and sold its gas interests to Amerada Hess.

Consumers were not well informed and had little awareness of how the gas industry worked and who would take responsibility for technical difficulties. Nor was it an easy matter to decide which company offered the best deal. Those on pre-payment meters however were being charged more than others, both by the incumbent and the new entrants. Unscrupulous sales techniques continued to be an anxiety. The regulator's workload had increased hugely. This aspect of it was quite new and Ofgas seemed slow to become involved on the side of the consumer. The regulator admitted to being 'completely blown over' by the problems (TIC, Session 1997–8, HC 338, p. 49). The complaint was made that gas consumers in the rest of the country were in effect subsidizing those who stayed with BG (CA, 1997, p. 119). BG's new ValuePlus tariff which introduced a further discount of 5.5 per cent was said by competitors to be predatory pricing, but it was cleared by Ofgas since competition was now said to be 'established,' albeit in one rather narrowly defined area of the market.

The problems of charging for water

Competition having been achieved in gas, electricity and telecoms, it still seemed far off for the water industry. Water has far more natural monopoly characteristics than gas and electricity. Littlechild's 1988 report on the industry for the government described it as 'the natural monopoly par excellence' (Littlechild, 1988, p. 44), or as *The Economist* put it, 'if you can privatize water, you can privatize anything' (8 Feb. 1986).

The new responsibility on the energy regulator to take into account the needs of low-income households has a parallel in the water industry even though the provisions in the Bill for water were withdrawn at an early stage. There is more cross subsidy; different payment methods do not attract different charges and frequent payment incurs no extra charge (Waddams Price, 2000).

In spite of a more commercial approach having been adopted in the 1970s and substantial increases in charges, there was after privatization a vast backlog of investment required to improve quality, cope with rising demand and comply with European directives. As a result, instead of the RPI−X formula, the water industry pricing was based on RPI+K; and customers saw their water bills rise year by year. This is why the regulator was determined to consult more widely and intensively than the other regulators and to get the customers involved, though this may be expecting too much in a 'market' in which the customer is not interested in the product until something goes wrong. As a result of the large increases which have taken place, the cost of water is of great importance to domestic consumers; and from the consumer's point of view a key difference between water and the other utilities which are delivered to the home by pipes or wires is the way water is charged for. It is based on rateable values (RV) for properties set in 1971. Only ten per cent of properties have water meters. Since for the vast majority the supply is unmeasured, the marginal cost is zero and there is no incentive to be economical. The household sector, which accounts for 60 per cent of the market, bears the brunt of the increases and once again this hits the lower income groups hardest since fixed charges are added to bills based on rateable values.

At the time of privatization, the policy was to continue with the rateable value basis only until March 2000. The poll tax fiasco may have made the devising of a new system more problematic, but at any rate the government decided in 1996 to extend the RV system beyond the deadline; a move unopposed by the Labour party. Basing charges on a system which is so out of date is fairly meaningless, but changing to a base on the current council tax would have the consequence of large increases to those in properties with low rateable values, in other words making the charges even more regressive than they are now.

The undoubted result of this would be a good deal of political unpopularity. It would also be expensive and would involve the release of council tax information to water companies, something the government was not prepared to do (*Utilities Journal*, April 1998, p. 17).

From some points of view metering is the obvious answer to these problems. But meters are costly to install[1] except in new houses and to read and maintain, so again competitive metering might hit the worse off hardest. On the other hand, especially where gardens are frequently watered and there are swimming pools, meters can cut consumption and might reduce the need to build reservoirs at huge capital cost, not to mention the price in public disapproval and environmental damage. Ian Byatt always supported metering and found a certain measure of public support for this. But in order not to charge metered customers far more than unmetered, rebalancing has had to take place, reducing the standing charge for those with meters so that their level of charges is more or less the same as the rest of the population (Vass, 1995d, pp. 70–1). Though most new houses now have meters and anyone can have one installed and change their mind within a year, progress towards universal metering is very slow: at the current rate there will still be 10 million unmetered households in 2050. The latest government policy is not to insist on compulsory meters but to use technology to develop more sophisticated tariffs and to abolish the standing charge for those who are on meters. In the long term metering is likely to be seen as the first best with compulsory metering in some properties (Harris, 1999, p. 107). A ban on disconnection means that further rebalancing has to take place to recover lost revenue. Once again, these pressures mean an attempt to reconcile conflicting objectives. It is difficult to move simultaneously towards cost reflective pricing and greater assistance to the disadvantaged. Measures to protect the vulnerable were introduced in 1999; low income customers on a metered supply who have three or more dependent children or certain medical conditions can apply for means-tested special help, but this has been criticized for imprecise targeting and lack of clarity.

The adoption of a piecemeal approach – the use of HEES, EESoPs, and joint initiatives with Transco – is evidence of the complexity of the problems of poverty. The companies cannot solve them, though they can be induced to devise easier payment schemes and to treat vulnerable customers with 'sensitivity'. Some companies are going further than this. TXU introduced in May 2000, under the slogan 'no bills, no debt, no queries', a social action tariff aimed at those in receipt of certain specified benefits. The charges were 20 per cent less than the customer had being paying previously and it was estimated that it would benefit a large proportion of households in fuel poverty. The abolition of the standing charge by BGT in 2000 was also presented as an aid to the low-income groups, but it can in fact only help those who use small amounts of fuel. Nor can the regulator provide solutions to housing and health problems. The new primary duty, however, alters the role fundamentally, away from the pursuit of efficiency towards the administering of distributive justice.

4
Monopoly and Competition

'If there is a market, regulators are redundant and if there is no market regulators do not know what to do.'*

Monopoly, the world famous board game of capitalist strategy, offers its players the opportunity to buy not only Park Lane or Leicester Square, but also to acquire an electric company, a water works or one of four railway stations. British players accustomed to monolithic nationalized utilities would until the 1980s have found this concept puzzling. But even when transferred to the private sector, each utility retained a substantial amount of monopoly power. More than fifteen years after the process of privatization began, public opinion remains hostile to the idea of these now private companies making large profits and paying their directors generous salaries. A few of these companies still retain their monopoly, but they are now bought and sold in a way that was not envisaged when they were privatized and the need to regulate market power and resolve disagreements over licences brings the utilities into the ambit of the MMC (now the Competition Commission) and the Office of Fair Trading.

British competition policy has never been so virulently anti-trust as that in the United States. Monopoly as such is not considered an offence, only its abuse is punishable. The Monopolies Commission was set up in 1948 and reform was long overdue by the time the new Competition Act was passed in 1998 to come into effect in 2000. Sir Gordon Borrie, a former Director General of Fair Trading, was stating the evident truth when he told the Trade and Industry Committee in 1994–5. 'For many years now, government policy towards the promotion

*Colin Robinson, 1996, p. 138.

of competition and the restraint of cartels and monopoly power has been marked by lack of will, dither and uncertainty' (TIC, Session 1994–5, HC 249, para. 69). Ten years had elapsed between a Conservative White Paper and the new Act; a draft bill had been dropped in 1996. This procrastination may also have been the reason for the premature resignation of his successor, Sir Bryan Carsberg (*Economist*, 20 April 1996). Furthermore, competition policy is conducted within an immensely complex network of relationships that are complicated still further by the newer features of the landscape, OFTEL, Ofgas, OFFER and Ofwat: so much so that the situation has been described as a 'regulatory Tower of Babel' (Wilks, 1994, p. 26). Duties, responsibilities and powers overlap and intertwine. The Competition Commission writes reports but also serves as an appeal body potentially investigating appeals about their own work. Labour government pledges to remove merger references from politics may alter the situation.

Most commentators have stressed the novelty of the utility regulators, but Stephen Wilks points out that there was at least as much continuity as innovation to be found in the design of the new Offices (Wilks, 1997). The format of the regulatory structure for the privatized utilities – as opposed to the price control formula discussed in chapter 1 – was substantially influenced by the model of competition policy that had existed for 25 years. This was based on the Monopolies and Mergers Commission and the Office of Fair Trading (OFT). Both these institutions operate administratively rather than judicially (Wilks, 1997, p. 8), and are intended to be at arms' length from government. The OFT shares with the utility regulators the same complex administrative relationship with ministerial departments, the MMC and other regulatory agencies. The essential feature of the system is that due to the limited powers entrusted to both MMC and OFT, it is the minister who decides how the public interest should be interpreted. The purpose of the system as it was originally established was to ensure an even-handed enquiry. The matter in hand was to be judged in terms of the public interest. The role of the Commission was always investigative and adjudicative, but it had no powers to initiate an enquiry, and would pass on the results of its investigations to the Board of Trade (or DTI) for a decision.

Its remit was to judge whether a monopoly (or later, a merger) would act against the public interest. The full time chairman is appointed by the Secretary of State; there are also up to fifty part-time members appointed initially for three years (and often renewed for another three) and three deputy chairmen. They may be academics, lawyers, trade union officials, businessmen or accountants. Very few are scientists or engineers. Of about 100 staff, headed by a secretary, approximately two-thirds are employees of the Commission and the rest are seconded from government departments and business. Like the commissioners they will probably be economists, lawyers, industrial experts and accountants. A panel of between three and six members conducts each enquiry with either the chairman or one of the deputies presiding; the secretary assigns a team of officials and sometimes uses outside advisers or consultants. Until 2000 there were special panels for telecoms, electricity, water and newspapers; there have now been replaced by a cross-utility panel. Though procedures are described as 'non-adversarial', legal representation is the norm at the 'hearings'. Commission members work for approximately a day and a half a week. This, it can be argued, is an amateur and part-time body, though many of the issues it has to investigate are highly technical. The terms of reference are wide and the panels vary in quality and experience. Though never popular, the MMC was a great survivor, an institution that was venerable without being distinguished. Virtually moribund in the early 1960s – the commission issued only 6 reports between 1958 and 1965 – its revival was triggered from the middle of the decade by new developments. First, in 1965 the Labour government (following a Conservative White Paper of 1964) added mergers to the Commission's responsibilities. Secondly, the merger boom of the 1970s, fuelled by competition among City firms, also contributed to a greater level of activity (Fairburn and Kay, 1989, p. 6).

Also instrumental in the renaissance of the Commission was the new Office of Fair Trading. Set up in 1973, and closely modelled on the US Federal Trade Commission (Ramsay, 1987, p. 176), it was partly a consumer protection agency and partly an agency for competition policy. The consumer side was intended to counter criticism from those who had opposed the abolition of the Consumer Council by the Conservative Government after the 1970 election. The OFT, which was said to have been inspired by Heath's new think tank (Ramsay, 1987, p. 180), was unusual in that responsibility was given to a named individual, inevitably referred to as a 'watchdog', or more formally Director General (DG). His main duties on the consumer side were to monitor markets and sift complaints. On the competition side he was to inform himself about monopolies and restrictive practices, which he might refer to the MMC. In the case of a merger, he had no power to make a direct reference to the MMC but advised the Secretary of State on whether it should be investigated. In a contentious case, this could be referred to a (formerly secret) mergers panel which collected the views of different interested government departments. The DGFT chaired this panel but his advice was not invariably followed (Fairburn and Kay, 1989, p. 7).

The DTI Competition Division also took an interest in all such cases: thus work was duplicated, but also presumably political control was reinforced. Once a report had come back from the MMC, the DGFT again had a role in advising the Secretary of State on whether or not it should be acted on. This hiatus in the proceedings gave an opportunity for lobbying for or against a reference, and the public interest criteria which were supposed to be the foundation of all the MMC's judgements gradually became wider. Finally in 1984 the 'Tebbit guidelines' were introduced: according to these, mergers should be referred to the Commission only on competition grounds (Fairburn and Kay, 1989, p. 7).

The system as it has evolved makes use of a separation of functions and checks and balances. If the OFT can be seen as the prosecutor and the judicial function belongs to MMC, the Secretary of State for Trade and Industry (or from 1991 to 1997, President of the Board of Trade) is the third corner of this triangle and exercises the executive function (Odgers, 1995, p. 3). He or she has considerably more power than most comparable ministers in other countries. Though the decision to refer remains in theory independent of the political process, and an MMC decision that a monopoly situation is not against the public interest is final, the minister can in other cases decide to ignore the MMC's recommendations and has no obligation to give reasons either for referring or not referring or for ignoring or rejecting MMC recommendations. Thus the situation is one of 'ultimate control by the political arm of government' (Craig, 1987, p. 217). Though there is a danger of arbitrariness here, it does as Graeme Odgers, former chairman of the MMC has conceded, allow the government to govern (Odgers, 1995, p. 6).

The OFT was intended to be a completely new kind of organization 'a pivotal development in relation to competition policy specifically and British policy on regulation more generally' (Wilks, 1994, p. 40) and was judged sufficiently successful to provide a template which more than a decade later gave shape to OFTEL and the other regulatory offices. The DG was 'a new player in the political game' (Ramsay, 1987, p. 181), even though his brief was a somewhat ambivalent one. The idea was that the OFT should be a non-civil service type of organization with plenty of outsiders and plenty of expertise in the technocratic style favoured by Heath. The DG was appointed for five years. Sir Gordon Borrie, the second to occupy the position (the first, Sir John

Methven, having died suddenly), had a background in consumer law and had been on the council of the CA and on the Equal Opportunities Commission. He had also stood, without success, as a Labour parliamentary candidate at the general elections of 1955 and 1959, and later, as Lord Borrie, was to become a member of Ofgem's advisory board.

Though neither Borrie nor his predecessor were civil servants, few other outsiders joined the OFT. Indeed under John Bridgeman (DGFT, 1996–2000), this was still the case and the three chief staff members below the DG were all civil servants, so it continued to resemble a government department. Many staff were seconded from the DTI, including the deputy director, though a high public profile was developed and the media were used extensively. Expertise was never very strong and the small size of the organization meant that limited career opportunities led to a high staff turnover. This was not the only problem; there is a dual tension between the twin duties of the DG as a defender of the consumer and a watchdog on competition policy and between his function as a technocrat and his role as a political player. Expertise is bound to take second place. It is worth repeating a remark by an American lawyer, Jaffe: 'the autonomy of expertness as an objective determinant of policy is, I am afraid, an illusion. Policy-making is politics' (Ramsay, 1987, p. 198). This statement is to be found in an article revealingly entitled 'The Independent Agency – a New Scapegoat'.

The MMC and OFT and the utilities

The role of the MMC and OFT in relation to the utilities has been of the greatest importance: the MMC has been the 'lynch pin' in ensuring companies' compliance with regulation (Helm, 1994a, p. 26). Like both of those offices, the regulators have few sanctions and a basically administrative modus operandi, though an adversarial element is introduced by the RPI − X formula.

The Commission deals with monopolies, mergers and anti-competitive practices under a variety of statutes and has carried out investigations of each of the utilities. The MMC becomes involved where a company cannot agree licence changes proposed by the regulator; and as always, the public interest test applies. This type of reference has been called the 'nuclear option', when regulator and company are quite unable to agree (Helm, TIC 1997, Memos, p. 122). An example of this is the continuing battle between the gas regulator and British Gas, which is described in detail later in this chapter. Most regulators can also refer their industries on monopoly grounds or in the case of anti-competitive practices. A monopoly reference would be under the Fair Trading Act 1973 and an anti-competitive practice reference under the Competition Act 1980. An example of the latter was the controversy over number portability in the telecommunications industry (1995). If there is an adverse finding the regulator must take the report into account but can generally make the final decision. The arrangements for water are rather different: in a reference concerning a licence amendment the Commission's decision is binding. Additionally a reference is obligatory for mergers over £30 million. This requirement was introduced shortly after privatization when two French utility companies acquired several small water only companies. Because competition in the industry was so remote, and Byatt was committed to comparing companies, there was a presumption against too much concentration from the start. The price review for airports owned by the British Airports Authority, which is regulated by the CAA, also goes compulsorily to the MMC every five years.

References to the Commission involving the utilities have over the first fifteen years or so been fewer than might have been expected.[1] Apart from references on price controls and other licence amendments, there were also in the mid- to late-1990s a number of takeovers and mergers in the electricity industry, which were referred by the Secretary of State. The sequence of events following a reference can become quite complicated. After the Commission has completed its enquiry and before the Secretary of State announces his decision, there is an opportunity for extensive lobbying and politicians may get involved. The Fair Trading Act has a very broad definition of the public interest and the OFT and MMC often disagreed on what it was. In evidence to a Trade and Industry Committee enquiry on monopolies the DGFT (Carsberg) told the committee that he defined it in terms of 'consumer well being'. The MMC chairman (Odgers) said it was impossible to define in a general context (TIC, 1994–5, para. 20). In fact so broad is it that it is difficult to exclude evidence. The public interest as defined by the MMC for a monopoly or merger enquiry includes the aims of maintaining and promoting competition, promoting the interests of consumers, the development of new products and reducing costs, a balanced distribution of industry and employment and promoting the competitiveness of British companies overseas – in other words almost everything. As a result, in the 1970s, the issues raised over mergers became more diverse, and the way they were treated increasingly politicised. Eventually target companies saw it as a worthwhile ploy to lobby for a reference as a delaying tactic. Hence the 'Tebbit guidelines'.

Though the Commission has tried hard to establish public interest standards, it has found this difficult and inconsistencies are evident between one report and another and (occasionally) dissenting opinions within the commission; an important case involving National Power and PowerGen is recounted below.

The framework in which the MMC has to work presents several problems. It is not bound by precedent, it is supposed to look 'at the specifics of the situation' (TIC, Session 1994–5, HC 249, para. 45). This means that it is frequently accused of inconsistency. Worse still, perhaps, being adjudicative, it is a totally reactive body; it cannot undertake an enquiry without its being referred, either by the secretary of state in the case of a merger situation or the DGFT in the case of a monopoly. Thus it has no control of its own workload. Furthermore, once a report is delivered to the Secretary of State, those members who are responsible for it have no further part to play and are thus 'totally detached from the decision-making process' (TIC, Session 1994–5, HC 249, para. 66). The DGFT on the other hand, who has taken no part in the investigation, though he may have referred it, is consulted.

More seriously perhaps, the MMC as a whole has 'no responsibility for developing a co-ordinated and on-going competition policy' (TIC, 1994–5, para. 46). Its methods of working are often regarded as unsatisfactory. Staff are variable in quality partly due to civil service pay constraints. The MMC is vulnerable to criticism about its lack of professionalism and sometimes its lack of speed. Doubt has also been cast on its procedures, which have been characterised as fragmented and even sloppy. Its custom has been to make enquiries, then hear evidence from the referred company and other interested parties. At the beginning of an investigation the members are 'wading through a paper mountain' (Odgers, 1995, p. 15). Apparently vast amounts of information are requested, some of which will already have been supplied to the OFT. Identification of the key issues can take several months and the completion of an enquiry can take anything from six to 12 months or even longer. This is partly no doubt because the commissioners are part-timers with other jobs, who have no other involvement than the specific enquiry they happen to be working on and whose attendance may of necessity be sporadic.

Consistency is maintained by the chairman and his deputies chairing all panels between them and meeting frequently. Though the rules of natural justice must be observed, the way the questioning goes, with members often assuming a devil's advocate role, means that those being investigated remain in the dark about the direction in which the enquiry is headed. Finally the panel proposes 'remedies'. Enquiries are not only time-consuming but also expensive. Costs of a single reference can exceed £1m and Scottish Hydro's 1995 reference was said to have been twice that (TIC, Session 1996–7, HC 50, p. 170).

Another type of criticism is on the question of transparency; the MMC has been described as an 'hermetically sealed institution' (*Times*, 10 April 1997). Although it publishes lengthy reports, which is transparency of a kind in a secretive world, many of the tables in reports have blank spaces to conceal sensitive figures. Not all the evidence it receives is made public and it publishes no verbatim records as for instance House of Commons Committees do. Even to the participants in an enquiry, confidentiality sometimes seems to be taken too far; the evidence of the other side is not usually available. OFTEL, like BT, preferred to avoid the Commission, because of its closed procedures. During the 1995 enquiry on number portability, the evidence of BT was not passed on to OFTEL (Hall et al., 2000, p. 93). On the other hand for some regulated utility companies, the MMC procedures are too open. Recently a little more light has been thrown upon the process. In 1999 a preliminary report was issued on share underwriting, the first time this had been done; but this approach could add as much as three months to a six-month enquiry. In 1998 the Commission held joint hearings of the main parties involved in the issue of mobile to mobile telecoms charges; this included OFTEL, BT, four other mobile network operators and consumer committees (Morris, 1998, p. 62). Though there is in theory no possibility of a resolution by negotiation it is likely that an element of this creeps in.

There is a view that academics are too influential. The chairman of the Competition Commission is an Oxford academic who has been a member and deputy chairman for years, so this is unlikely to alter. Though part time appointments have their disadvantages, they can attract a wide range of expertise that would not otherwise be available. This expertise, as Beesley pointed out, when he was himself a member, would not be available in the High Court (Beesley, 1994, p. 151). The freedom of action of the DTI on the receipt of an MMC report raises questions about accountability and fairness. The Secretary of State can alone decide not to refer any qualifying merger, and he alone can prohibit one. He can do this even if the MMC decides that it would not operate against the public interest. Michael Heseltine when in office argued that he should have the power to decide on remedies because the Secretary of State is accountable to parliament for decisions on matters of public interest. But where the Secretary of State opposes the

MMC decision and substantial change is recommended, it is increasingly thought that the decision should be subject to parliamentary approval and he should give his reasons.

The interwoven connections familiar to students of British government are particularly striking in the MMC/OFT/DTI nexus. Professor Michael Beesley was described as a sort of 'godfather' of regulators, and as was pointed out in Chapter 1, a close colleague of Professor Stephen Littlechild, the electricity regulator and an adviser at OFFER. Other names which recur in this small area of activity are John Bridgeman, recently Director General of Fair Trading, and Colin Robinson, formerly Professor at Surrey University, leading light of the IEA and enthusiast for the 'gale of creative destruction' envisaged by Schumpeter. Robinson is, interestingly, married to Eileen Marshall, who divided her recent working life between OFFER and Ofgas and then became a deputy director of Ofgem. Littlechild, Beesley, Robinson and Bridgeman among others were all members of the MMC as well as their other regulatory commitments, and the first two were also on the panel for the gas enquiries in 1987 and 1992 respectively. Subsequently Beesley was appointed a special adviser to both OFFER and Ofgas. The regulatory web is indeed tightly woven (*Times*, 24 Aug. 1994): all of these people were influential in the fate of the gas industry after it was privatized.

The British Gas story

When privatized in 1986, British Gas was the largest company in the FTSE 100 Index, one of the largest companies in Europe, highly profitable and fully integrated from exploration and production right through to domestic supply and appliances, though a monopoly only from 'beachhead to meter'. It had 90,000 employees, 16.5 million tariff customers and 20,000 contract customers.[2] Not only did the company operate right across the industry but it also bought all North Sea gas on 25-year contracts.

The natural gas industry has four stages: production (getting it out of the sea, mainly done by oil companies), piping it to the beach head, transmission through a high pressure network and low pressure distribution to the customer. The middle two stages both have natural monopoly characteristics, but for competition in supply all that is needed is access to the network. Price competition should in theory be strong, since it is a homogeneous product, in spite of some customers in the south west during the pilot stage of competition 'noticing a change in colour' when they changed supplier. One cubic metre of gas is pretty much like another, and indeed is required to be, so that the system can be operated safely. Safety is an important consideration, since gas does not 'fail safe' as electricity usually does, but fails to danger. Variations in demand are very large – demand on a cold winter's day can be five times that on a summer day – so storage is important. Gas lines can be packed and empty fields filled, but the existence of an 'interruptible' market also helps deal with variations in demand. In spite of these, peak pricing is not used, as is widely the case in electricity and telecoms, partly for technical reasons and partly because of the cost of metering. Traditionally, uniform pricing resulted in cross-subsidies and there were discounts for large contracts.

British Gas moved from the public to the private sector as an integrated monopoly. Its social obligations were less than those imposed on BT. There was no restructuring of the industry partly because the sell-off timetable was tight if the government was to complete it before the next election and consequently the DTI depended greatly on British Gas technology and expertise. No White Paper was issued and the industry was given an extremely light regulatory regime; the possibility of competition in the larger industrial market pre-existed but there was at that time no intention of introducing it into the domestic market. An amendment sponsored by Michael Portillo inserted into the 1986 Gas Act a general duty to promote competition and British Gas had to publish indications of the cost of using the network. This was to prove a vital weapon for the regulator over the first few years. The 1982 Oil and Gas (Enterprise) Act had made third party access to the pipelines theoretically possible but such was the dominant position of British Gas that it had no practical effect. At privatization the company controlled as much as 60 per cent of the domestic energy market, 75 per cent in areas where gas was available, and 36 per cent of the industrial market (T. Jones, 1993, p. 113). The struggle to introduce competition into this monolithic corporation was to take more than ten years and several references to the MMC as well as monitoring by the OFT.

Perhaps not surprisingly, the newly privatized company continued to behave as it always had done. Having been secretive for many years, it continued to act in character. Complaints from industrial customers about price discrimination started very soon after privatization. Prices to these large customers, who took more than 25,000 therms a year, were unregulated but represented almost 40 per cent of sales by volume (T. Jones, 1993, p. 117). Though oil prices were falling, they saw no reductions. British Gas was negotiating confidential, individual contracts, charging more to those who could not easily use coal, oil or electricity and refusing cheaper interruptible contracts to those who could. Their complaints led to a reference to the MMC by the DGFT in 1987.

British Gas, supported by the government, argued to the MMC that there was sufficient competition in the contract market for regulation to be unnecessary, even though the company had more than 30 per cent of the total fuel market. But the MMC found there was discrimination and a lack of transparency. BG was ordered to publish a schedule of prices and access terms for competitors and to contract for only 90 per cent of each new field. The OFT, in an unusual arrangement, was to keep an eye on developments and report back to the MMC in three years. If the company failed to lose enough market share, it would be penalised further (Waddams Price, 1997b, p. 53). By 1991, however, circumstances had radically changed. New gas supplies had been discovered and the EC had lifted its ban on the use of gas for electricity generation and also introduced more stringent limits on sulphur dioxide emissions. As a result, gas fired power stations using CCGT technology developed in the US in the late 1980s, which emitted virtually no sulphur, became an attractive option, especially since a carbon energy tax was under discussion by the EC. The regulator welcomed this as it might counter the market power of the privatized electricity generators (Green and Newbery, 1997, p. 35).

Robert Evans had by now succeeded Denis Rooke as chairman of British Gas; but relations between the company and Ofgas continued to be less than cordial. The OFT's review of the market situation found that although British Gas had kept to the agreement specified by the MMC, competition was still not at the sustainable stage. Would-be competitors still had little or no access to gas supplies, British Gas's monopoly in the tariff market continued and its control of transportation and storage remained. British Gas also undercut its rivals in the interruptible market. Accordingly, the OFT among many recommendations, required the surrender of 60 per cent of the bulk market and a reduction of the tariff market threshold to below 2,500 therms. Far more fundamental however, was the recommendation that access to the transport and storage system must be permitted if competition was ever to develop properly (Armstrong et al., 1994, p. 263). Separation into two businesses – transportation and storage and supply – under the same ownership was also recommended. Huge amounts of time and effort were to be expended over the next few years to achieve this.

This constituted a change from regulation of conduct to regulation of the structure of the industry.

Lengthy negotiations ensued and the separation of supply from transportation and storage was scheduled for September 1992, but later postponed for a year. After this the market share of the incumbent fell fast, but the failure of Ofgas and British Gas to agree on a rate of return for the transportation system resulted in a new double MMC reference in 1992. British Gas asked the President of the Board of Trade to refer the whole business under the Fair Trading Act and Ofgas sought an investigation of transportation and storage and the fixing of tariffs under the Gas Act.

During the enquiry a certain amount of information was leaked about the submissions by the various parties, some of it rather contentious, a pattern that was to be repeated in 1996. Early in the proceedings, McKinnon told the Commission that BG was not one monopoly but three – purchasing, transport and supply. The pipeline was the only natural monopoly, in his opinion. This received an 'apoplectic' reaction from British Gas, and City commentators now saw McKinnon as being clearly on the side of the consumer, and perceived the government as having failed to spell out to the regulators precisely what their role was.

Evidence from the DTI, which was very brief, stressed that 'breaking up would be hard to do', and that separation would require new legislation. They also argued that overseas expansion might be jeopardized (Stern, 1994, p. 24) and that the government's commitment to opening the tariff market could not easily be combined with divestment. The shippers had argued that competition in the non-tariff market alone could not be sustained. British Gas opposed this since it took the view that that abolishing the monopoly in the tariff market could compromise safety and security of supply. The 1,000-page report, which came out in August 1993, was widely seen as more thorough and thoughtful than the previous one. Competition in the non-tariff market was by now having an effect. The key decision, perhaps not entirely unexpected after hints dropped by the OFT two years previously, was that the structure of the industry contained an inherent conflict of interest. The Commission made it clear that in its opinion – and one of the members of the panel was Michael Beesley – the fact that BG was both a seller of gas and the owner of the only transportation system made the development of genuine competition more difficult. A neutral network was essential. Also essential was the removal of the monopoly in the tariff market. This, it had already been made clear by the government, was a firm intention. The MMC recommended an initial further fall in the tariff/contract boundary to 1,500 therms in 1997 (which would bring competition to 400,000 homes and 100,000 businesses) but took a cautious approach to the complete abolition of the monopoly, partly because it would require legislation. Separation of the transportation system would improve the amount of information available to the regulator. The Commission also accurately foresaw the issues that would be raised by competition in the domestic market – the unravelling of cross subsidies likely once real competition in supply came into effect, as a result of 'cherry-picking' and similar practices.

These were the arguments. However, it was a full four months before the government made any public reaction to the Commission's report and in the meantime circumstances altered. The nine-month period of the MMC enquiry and the consultation period, which followed, were characterized by a complex series of political cross currents and conflicting influences, which illustrated the interdependence of the various elements in the energy sector. It also demonstrated once again how opposition on government backbenches, especially when the majority has been whittled down, really can block some policies.

There were several factors at work that could potentially influence the government's decision on the gas industry. In the City there was anxiety about breaking the regulatory contract that had been agreed at privatization. There were still two million small shareholders, the so-called 'Sids' who had bought shares for the first time at flotation. The sale of the third and last tranche of BT shares, worth £5 billion, was due to take place in the summer of 1993 and the time allowed for the MMC report on gas was extended to permit this to take place before publication. The DTI report on the coal industry that appeared in January 1993 proposed the slowing of CCGT construction. The remaining 40 per cent of the shares in the electricity generators were also due to be sold in 1995 but they too could be affected by the uncertainty in the coal industry. Gas and oil producers were anxious that employment in their industries might be threatened. There was also considerable anxiety about the impact of rising fuel prices especially after the announcement of the introduction of VAT on fuel. Another privatization issue that was lurking in the background during the enquiry was the Post Office, the future of which was being reviewed by the government. The plan to sell it aroused considerable opposition.

During the period of the enquiry the gas shippers launched a PR campaign designed to encourage the government to open the market. The RECs also favoured this. The British Gas line had altered somewhat; it would undertake internal separation of businesses and consider domestic competition. The idea of a complete split was opposed for reasons of international competition. The company had skilfully positioned itself as a world player by means of a powerful advertising campaign and had convinced the DTI of the strength of its arguments. Other changes were taking place; the new gas regulator Clare Spottiswoode took over from James McKinnon in November 1993 and Cedric Brown was due to take over at British Gas. The arrival of Richard Giordano as chairman of the company was to mark a change in its approach.

A major complication in the situation was the heart attack suffered by Michael Heseltine, the President of the Board of Trade, in June 1993, just at the moment when the report was said to be complete and ready to go to the DTI. It was not clear whether Tim Sainsbury, who was deputising for him and might favour a big world role for British Gas, or Tim Eggar, the energy minister, would take the decision. The latter, who had a background in the oil and gas business, had taken a tough line over the reduction of the threshold for the tariff market in 1992, and might have been expected to favour the independents. In the event months went by and nothing happened.

No decision was announced till just before Christmas, after parliament had risen for the recess. Heseltine, by now back at work, knew that it would be difficult to reject the MMC report completely. One person who had been a critic of the original 1986 Gas Act was Michael Portillo, by this time Chief Secretary to the Treasury. The dilemma of aiming on the one hand to prevent a rise in prices to domestic consumers especially in view of the impending VAT on fuel imposed by Lamont's 1993 budget, and on the other of wanting to increase competition made things still trickier. At this point it still seems to have been widely believed (and it was a point of view enthusiastically promoted by British Gas) that competition would result in price rises for consumers because of the consequent erosion of cross-subsidies. British Gas suggested that for some low-income customers gas prices might almost double (MMC, 1993, p. 356).

When Heseltine finally announced his decision on the MMC report in December 1993, he rejected the main recommendation on divestment, saying that separation of businesses under British Gas ownership should take place instead. The company was divided up into five units in March 1994, having been preparing for this for some time. Secondly, far from moving slowly towards competition in the domestic market, he announced that it would begin in April 1996 and be completed two years later. This decision was probably determined at least partly by electoral considerations: an election was very likely to take place in 1997 and it would be better to have any teething troubles over beforehand. Also the RECs were due to be liberalized by 1998, though they would have had eight years of moving towards competition and it had been planned for in the legislation. By comparison, gas competition was being rushed through; on the other hand to stall it would contradict the principle enunciated in the White Paper on the future of the coal industry that competition should be encouraged and customers given choice. Complete divestment would constitute an admission that the 1986 scheme was flawed and might have been seen as a breaking of the implicit bargain made at privatization.

A new Act of Parliament was needed to put the decision into practice but there was some difficulty in finding room for it in the legislative programme. It came down to a choice between the Gas Bill and the Post Office Bill. Clare Spottiswoode was pressing hard for the former to go ahead. So too was British Gas, where Giordano the new chairman had perceived that both regulatory clarity and management focus would be improved by a complete separation. New legislation would create different licences and make demerger possible. The Post Office Bill would have raised funds for the Treasury, reduced the PSBR and supplied the opportunity for a pre-election tax cut, but there was also entrenched opposition to the plan throughout the country and a determined, and ultimately successful, campaign to stop it. Cabinet was divided on the issue, but it was decided by 12 Conservative backbenchers who refused to support the government on the Post Office Bill, a further humiliation for the Major government. As a result the Gas Bill found its place in the November 1994 Queen's speech; immediately, the structure of domestic tariffs began to change, with the introduction of discounts for direct debit payers.

As the previous chapter explained, competition began in the south west in April 1996, pushed through by the DTI and Ofgas. It had been evident for some time and indeed had been foreseen by the MMC, that the question of cross-subsidies could cause major political difficulties. This issue had been left to Ofgas to deal with and it was examined again by the Trade and Industry committee in the autumn of 1994, before the bill was passed. The smaller gas companies waiting to get into the domestic market were delighted at Heseltine's decision. Eastern Group, describing itself as the second biggest energy supplier in the UK, stoutly argued that if cherry picking were to take place it would be proof that 'the cherries are being overcharged' (TIC, Session 1994–5, HC 23-II, pp. 3–6). The Consumers Association also favoured the move to competition. Falling gas prices for the entrants permitted them to offer discounts on the prices British Gas was charging based on long term contracts. The take or pay contracts which the company had entered into were at higher prices than the new entrants were paying – so the latter were not necessarily more efficient. British Gas whose corporate culture was notable for its inertia, had not expected competition to arrive so soon and had signed contracts before privatization in 1986 and before 1993 when the government had decided to open up the market. By the end of 1995, the spot price for gas was 10 p per therm, as opposed to the 20 p British Gas was paying (*Economist*, 28 Oct. 1995).

The 1996 MMC reference

Transportation prices were once again the triggering factor for a further MMC reference in 1996. The company had by now set in train a split along the lines recommended by the MMC in 1993, that is a complete separation in ownership, not just a separation of businesses as before. It was divided into Centrica, which took downstream supply and servicing and the Morecambe field; and Transco, which had the pipeline business, exploration and production. For the next price review, a cap was agreed with Centrica, but Transco refused Spottiswoode's proposal for their prices. The central and most controversial issue here was the proposal to slash the value of the asset base to £12 billion, compared with Transco's figure of £17 billion. This was the result of altering the method of calculation used in 1993 and would imply a price cut of over 20 per cent. It was described by British Gas as 'the biggest smash and grab raid in history', and was what finally ensured a reference to the MMC, but not before the company had mounted a PR campaign to try and change the regulator's mind. The lobbying effort included encouraging shareholders to write in to Ofgas, and 35,000 did so, complaining that the proposals tilted the balance too far away from the shareholders and towards the customers. Institutional investors had also had meetings with Ofgas. At the same time, the other firms in the market, which used the pipelines and paid Transco's prices, were pressing for a larger cut in the charges.

As always, mutual suspicion was the most noticeable feature of relations between Ofgas and British Gas. A revised set of proposals, which the regulator claimed represented substantial concessions, was no more acceptable. Since they would mean a reduction in returns to shareholders, a reference to the MMC was inevitable.

There was now the prospect of a Labour government coming to power. Indeed the timetable for the MMC enquiry was extended to avoid the publication of the report in the middle of an election campaign. Originally due in April 1997, it eventually came out in June, after the election. The Ofgas proposals brought the regulator into conflict not only with Richard Giordano, but also with Ian Byatt the water regulator. He disagreed with the Spottiswoode approach to depreciation, and thus seemed to be lending aid to British Gas.

Before the report was published Spottiswoode made it clear that she might not implement all the Commission's findings. She was adamant that the way the previous investigation in 1993 had calculated the value of the pipeline system had resulted in higher charges than were justified, and would make it more difficult to open up other activities, such as meter installation and storage, to competition (*Financial Times*, 28 June 1987).

By the time the report came out in June 1997, the demerger of Centrica and Transco had taken place. The 400-page document endorsed the regulator's proposals. Game, set and match to Ms Spottiswoode, said the press. 'The MMC backed us on virtually all philosophical issues,' said Ms Spottiswoode. The Commission thus once again supported the regulator. The decision to value the pipelines and its ancillary parts at less than the company wanted was justified on the grounds that the 1993 findings represented regulatory thought 'at an early stage' (*Financial Times*, 18 June 1987). The Commission was said to have agonised over its recommendations; it reduced X to 2 per cent, and put forward the view that the cost of capital in such a low risk industry should be in the region of 7 per cent. But they also gave the company leeway to make efficiency savings. British Gas accepted the report with reasonably good grace, though they had spent £10 million and an enormous amount of management time on it; the deputy chairman, Philip Rogerson, quickly resigned.

The MMC has played a crucial role in encouraging compliance with the regulators. Clearly the major cases have been those involving British Gas, since the gas industry was frequently in the dock in Carey Street (home of the bankruptcy court as well as the MMC) between 1987 and 1997. It is at least arguable that this deterred other companies from seeking MMC referrals, particularly since the Commission mostly supported the regulators and usually favoured the introduction of competition.

After the 1994 price reviews for water and electricity, only two water companies, South West Water and Portsmouth Water, appealed to the

MMC. The electricity generator Scottish Hydro also did so. In these cases too the commission supported the water and electricity regulators. The two water cases were dealt with together, and parts of the reports are identical. The threat of a reference has been known to bring companies into line. Littlechild forced National Power and PowerGen to dispose of 6,000 MW of plant and a cap on pool prices or face an enquiry. Before that the pool had been unregulated and it is unlikely that the MMC would have recommended such regulation. Later, in 1996, the NGC decided to accept a tough review without appealing to the Commission because, it was said, they were busy developing Energis, their telephone company and could not spare the management time.

Utility mergers and acquisitions

Price reviews are only part of the Commission's work with utilities. In its capacity as the main instrument of competition policy together with the OFT, it considers whether mergers are in the public interest. Apart from the small water companies taken over by French utility companies, there was little activity in the utility sector immediately after privatization because of the golden shares, which expired in 1995. Later, there were other takeovers and attempted takeovers in the water industry. The key thing about water, as Chapter 2 described, was the importance of yardstick or comparative competition. To make this effective, the regulator needs as much information as possible on each company and a wide range of companies in order to keep tabs on each one. An important influence in what happened in this area was Byatt's commitment to the concept. But some water mergers were acceptable, for instance the one between North East Water and Northumbrian (January 1996). The former was already owned by Lyonnaise des Eaux and though the MMC felt it would operate against the public interest, Byatt decided that a substantial reduction in charges could make up for the loss.

More controversial was the case of South West Water. This was probably the company with the highest charges and biggest problems in the whole country. Both Wessex Water, based in Bristol, and Severn Trent (Birmingham) made bids for it and both were referred to the MMC. It recommended blocking both bids, as Ian Byatt had advised in evidence. To Byatt at least, committed to it though he undoubtedly was, comparative competition was evidently a complex concept: to maintain it, companies geographically close should not merge – so a merger of

Wessex and SWW would not be acceptable. Relative company size also had to be taken into account, so that other companies did not lose a comparator. Severn Trent was the second largest water company and merged with SWW would have been even larger than Thames and therefore a dangerous concentration would have been created. It would also have deprived Thames of a comparator. A further consideration for the water regulator was diversity of management style. The companies taken over by one of the French groups all seemed to manage their businesses in the same way (CA, 1997, pp. 213–14).

The water regulator stated 'No remedy even in the shape of a significant price cut would be sufficient to compensate for the loss of SWW as a comparator', and argued in favour of diversity of ownership, 'to secure the greatest variety of management styles and techniques' (Cowan, 1997, p. 85). Ian Lang, by now President of the Board of Trade since Heseltine had become deputy prime minister, decided to follow the MMC's view on this, which came as a great surprise to the bidding companies and the City. When launching their bids in spring 1996, both Wessex Water and Severn Trent considered they had a reasonable chance of success. Reports in the press suggested that Byatt would have allowed a Wessex bid with larger price cuts, but the MMC felt more strongly and Lang backed them. Byatt endorsed the decision. Comparative competition notwithstanding, a comment made by the chief executive of Severn Trent was that to focus on regulatory issues at the expense of benefits to customers was extraordinary (*Times*, 26 Oct. 1996). Should the industry and investors have interpreted this decision as ruling out further mergers?

The question was answered in the affirmative three months later when in January 1997 Lang decided that the proposal from two French water companies, Generale des Eaux and Saur to take over a small English 'water only' company, Mid Kent, (which they planned to split between their owned companies South East Water and Folkestone and Dover) was not acceptable. This was presented as an environmentally friendly merger since it would postpone the need to build a reservoir. The Secretary of State, the regulator and the MMC all had no difficulty in deciding that the deal should not be allowed to proceed, and the decision was supported by the Labour party. The reaction from the City and environmentalists was one of puzzlement, perhaps because some smaller mergers (Bournemouth and West Hants in January 1992; East Worcestershire acquired by Severn Trent in September 1993 and East Surrey and Sutton in October 1995) had been permitted (*Financial Times*, 22 Jan. 1997). But there were only five independent water only companies left, and Mid Kent had, under pressure from the hostile approach, improved its level of service enormously.

Littlechild's original theoretical framework (Littlechild, 1988) had argued that one of the principal points in favour of privatization was that inefficient firms would face the threat of takeover. But as Waterson has pointed out, there is a trade off between allowing takeovers to encourage productive efficiency and keeping enough firms in existence to permit cross-company comparisons (Waterson, 1995, p. 137). Other merger and acquisition activity took the form of creating multi-utilities, mixing electricity and water companies. Unlike water, in the electricity industry a reference to the MMC for a merger is not compulsory. But the electricity regulator was consulted by the DGFT and he had an important role to play in ensuring not only the protection of customers but also the ring fencing of assets (Prosser, 1997, pp. 169). The first multi-utility, United Utilities, was formed in 1995 by the purchase of Norweb by North West Water, which received a good deal of press attention on account of boardroom disputes and large executive salaries. Lang did not take the advice of John Bridgeman, the new DGFT, that this should be referred to the Commission. Hyder, the Welsh multi-utility, was created when Welsh Water bought SWALEC in 1996. The fact that these were not referred to the MMC was a matter of regret to ONCC – and possibly to Byatt as well. A bid by Southern Electric for Southern Water was blocked in 1996, which allowed Scottish Power, a highly integrated company which also owns Manweb, to come in and this too was nodded through. Because mergers in water over £30 million must go to the Commission, the bidder has to make the case and offer real efficiency improvements. The Scottish Power takeover of Southern Water in 1996 was permitted on condition that prices were cut (Prosser, 1997, p. 138; Weeden, 1996, p. 103).

The most striking and controversial series of acquisitions, however, was within the electricity sector. Within three months of the expiry of the golden shares, three bids had been launched, and by early 1997 ten out of the twelve RECs had been taken over, seven by US companies,[3] two, as mentioned, by water companies and one, Eastern, by Hanson. The Secretary of State had confirmed in August 1995 that each case would be considered on its merits and he would continue to refer proposed mergers to the MMC primarily on competition grounds, and listen to the advice of both the DGFT and the appropriate regulator. But these various parties did not always take the same view. For instance in the Manweb case, Littlechild wanted the merger to go to the MMC but the Secretary of State refused (Prosser, 1997, p. 170).

The two big generators, National Power and PowerGen, perhaps encouraged by this attitude, each attempted to acquire a REC, the first making a bid for Southern and the second for Midlands Electricity in September 1995. Both Southern and Midlands were active in the generation market, in common with all but one of the RECs, and had invested in CCGT plant. These attempts by the generators to reverse the disintegration of the industry, which had been imposed in the privatization act, were sent to the Commission by Lang. The sheer size of the companies involved must have been a factor, but the referral still came as a blow to the City and the companies. Lang was also no doubt sensitive to the bad publicity utility managers had attracted – an area where Labour criticisms hit home.

The MMC report, written under the chairmanship of Odgers, head of the MMC, concluded that the mergers, were they to go ahead, would not be in the public interest, but decided on balance that they should be permitted since they would make the companies more competitive in the international market. Domestically, the extent of competition and its potential effect remained uncertain and unquantifiable: on the generation side it could only reduce the power of other RECs to compete (CA, 1997, p. 212). A minority report by Patricia Hodgson, director of policy and planning at the BBC, voiced the opinion that there was already too little competition. She pointed out that the two big generators would continue to own the majority of non-baseload plant, further integration might be encouraged and entry discouraged. The electricity regulator saw no significant benefits in the merger, which was far larger than the Scottish Power–Manweb linkup. On the contrary, it would increase the market power of National Power and PowerGen and increase their incentive to control prices in the pool. The majority report was criticized for failing to provide a detailed examination of the industry's cost and price structure and devoting only two paragraphs to the issue of consumer prices (*Economist*, 13 April 1996). Odgers' known view that destroying strong interests would weaken 'UK plc' may have had an influence on this report. The verdict of the Consumers' Association was that this underlined the weakness and opacity of the MMC process; it is hard to disagree.

The equivocal nature of the MMC's report meant that Lang in deciding to block the mergers appeared to overrule the Commission.[4] The widespread expectation had been that he would endorse its recommendations. The markets had clearly anticipated that the deal would go through since the Scottish Power and Hanson bids had earlier been given the green light; £1 billion was wiped off electricity shares. The government said it would block any such bids until the market had become more competitive. But with only one independent REC, Southern, remaining, the idea of comparative competition did not seem very convincing. Once again, political pressures may have played a part. Disaffected Conservatives on the right of the party, including Lamont and Redwood, assuming the deals were going to go through, attacked the MMC and the government. For the Opposition, Gordon Brown prepared a motion criticizing the government for putting interests of powerful monopolies above those of consumers, which was never delivered since the decision went the other way (*Economist*, 27 April 1996). The MMC had not distinguished itself.

A measure of vertical integration was permitted in the case of Eastern, which bought some coal-fired stations which NP and PG had been forced to sell. These manoeuvres in the battle for corporate control in the electricity sector were not referred to the MMC, but instead assurances were sought in order to maintain the flow of information to the regulator. The regulator himself apparently saw them as a welcome increase in competition in generation.

PowerGen immediately sold its 21 per cent stake in Midland Electricity to a US company. Over the next few months most of the remaining independent RECs were also bought by American utility companies. SWEB had been sold in September 1995; East Midlands was next, then Northern and London were targeted and each time no referral took place, though the Northern bid was controversial and contested. Occasionally, there was an indication that the series of bids might be held up. In November 1996, for example, the OFT took some time to decide whether it should recommend a reference of the hostile take over bid by CE Electric for Northern Electric. CE's majority partner, Calenergy, was junk rated in the US, but managed to reassure the regulator. Finally, early in 1997 Yorkshire Electricity was bought by American Power, a deal that was done with great speed, since the election was so close that the date was practically fixed. So then there was one…Southern Electric considered itself the most efficient in the world and had reduced its controllable costs by half since 1991.

A major factor behind the American bids was a wish to become involved in the competitive electricity and gas markets after 1998; to leave behind the regulatory straitjacket at home in the US, to gain a foothold in Europe and acquire experience of the UK system which was gaining popularity overseas. Thus the Tebbit guidelines which had held for so long were beginning to be superseded.

Once the election was over and Labour returned to power a bid was referred, not on competition but on regulatory grounds. This was the Pacificorp bid for The Energy Group. Having been demerged from Hanson together with extensive coal interests in the US, the former Eastern Group presented an attractive target for several US corporations. The new President of the Board of Trade, Margaret Beckett, said that it might be 'harder to regulate if owned by an American company'. Since in opposition she had called for other such bids to be referred, she would have been open to accusations of hypocrisy or worse had she not done so. It was done against the advice of OFFER and the OFT. The issues involved were thus aired for the first time; at privatization there had been no expectation that this series of takeovers would happen. There seemed to be several anxieties. Apart from the debt burden of the purchasing company, there was the fact that once the market was opened up to competition – due in 1998, but subject to serious delays – distribution and supply would be separated, which might be seen as a breach of contract by the owning companies. Ring fencing of accounts has to be very good. What would happen if a company quarrelled with the regulator? US regulatory habits are very different. Littlechild told the MMC that the loss of an undiversified REC would be much more harmful than The Energy Group which had many non-electric interests. But the go-ahead for that bid reopened once more the question of vertical integration.

Though the deal was passed, the American company was later outbid by Texas Utilities (TXU). This seemed to give a positive signal to PowerGen, determined to acquire a REC at last. By the middle of 1998, when Mandelson replaced Beckett, PowerGen had an agreed deal with East Midlands Electricity, a US owned REC, and made it clear that selling off some of its power stations would be a price worth paying. There was disagreement between the regulator, the OFT and the Secretary of State on how much generating capacity should be shed. Littlechild wanted 6 GW, but would not oppose a takeover provided customers benefited. He was pressed by the DTI to reduce this requirement, since the department wanted to avoid an MMC reference. Bridgeman was in favour of a reference. This would have delayed the disposals and signing of long term coal contracts (*Times*, 25 Sep. 1998). All of these arrangements were delayed by problems over emissions permits.

Similarly, when National Power bought the supply business of Midland Electric agreeing to sell Drax, the advice of the electricity regulator and the DGFT was once more ignored. Meantime, other mergers were going ahead. EdF bought London Electricity, the second US-owned REC to be resold, and British Energy bought Swalec from Hyder. Efforts by Mandelson to get an MMC reference for this deal were not successful; it was cleared by Brussels in two months. SWEB later went to London Electricity, making EdF the first company to own two RECs. Failure to refer this acquisition is perhaps the most surprising of all. The MMC had no opportunity to examine these mergers and by the end of 1999 the electricity industry looked quite different with several major generators and a marked degree of integration. ScottishHydro and Southern Electric also merged. More consolidation among RECs was thought possible, but concerns remained about the effectiveness of competition in generation. The gas moratorium had strengthened the power of the large generators and the reform of the electricity trading arrangements (RETA, later NETA) was proving more problematic than had been expected.

Telecoms

The one area which has not been mentioned so far is that of telecoms. BT has largely avoided any entanglement with the MMC on licence changes or on monopoly grounds; its proposed merger with Canadian firm Mitel in 1986 was passed. It was suggested by Sir Gordon Borrie that BT's determination to avoid the Commission was due to its fear of being subjected to 'death by 1,000 cuts' which had been inflicted on the gas industry (Borrie, 1993, p. 61). There were no references under the first DG of OFTEL, Bryan Carsberg, though it came close in the quality crisis of 1987, and a reference was threatened. Under the second, Don Cruickshank, there were two, one concerned with the narrow issue of chatlines.

The second was the issue of number portability, the lack of which constituted a serious barrier to entry. The question to be decided was how the costs incurred were to be allocated. BT probably delayed the regulator for two years while the cable industry was developing (CA, 1997, p. 179). The matter was referred to the MMC in April 1995 and was essentially won by OFTEL but further negotiations over changes in the licence meant that the barriers came down only in June 1996. An agreement on number portability was reached in December 1997 and was gradually made available by other operators. In 1996, too, the regulator won a battle on anti-competitive practices. OFTEL wanted to put a fair trading condition into telecoms licences, and couple this with a lighter regime on prices, thus trading competition policy off against regulation (Currie, 1997, p. 3). BT objected that no right of appeal would exist if it were incorporated in the licence. In August 1996 BT sought judicial review, while accepting the more generous price control, in preference to going to the MMC; the court decided in OFTEL's favour in December 1996. OFTEL's ambition to become or be seen as a competition authority was well known. Such fair trading conditions are likely to become part of the armoury of other regulators. Ofgem's 1999 introduction of a good behaviour clause for the electricity generators was finally acceptable to all but two of them and was therefore referred to the Commission by them.

The telecommunications industry apart, judicial review has played a tiny part in competition policy. It first came into sharp focus when the Northern Ireland regulator, who deals with both electricity and gas (OFREG) decided to ignore the MMC recommendations which reduced his proposed cut in Northern Ireland Electricity (NIE) electricity distribution prices from 29 to 25 per cent. The company wanted 22 per cent, and sought a judicial review. Initially, NIE won against the regulator, but the High Court in Belfast found that the regulator McIldoon was entitled to make the licence amendments. A further appeal found that the regulator could not cut the company's revenue to less than the amount required to finance the business – a licence requirement. This judgement thus supported the MMC, in that the regulator must not move too far from its recommendations. So far this case is unique. The gas regulator, Clare Spottiswoode did however make an attempt to follow in McIldoon's footsteps in July 1997, when she indicated a disinclination to accept the MMC's proposals on gas transport and storage on a point of detail. Like McIldoon, she argued that it would result in smaller reductions to consumers and hence she would be failing in her duty if she accepted it. A compromise was reached (Howe, 1998, p. 216).

The NIE case was a first in two ways: the first time a regulator had not accepted the MMC role as an arbitrator and the first time the courts had been used in this way in the utility sector and raised queries about the standing of the MMC, already somewhat damaged by the apparent inconsistency over the previous two years or so, and about the vagueness of the legislation. Technically regulators may reject the conclusions of the MMC – the legal position is not clear. But if this happens, not only is the Competition Commission redundant, but even more power shifts to the regulator. The Utilities Act includes a requirement that the Commission's remedies should be followed.

The new Competition Act

The NIE submission argued that the MMC was 'a recognised court of appeal'. This is not really the case since the Commission simply gathers facts and issues recommendations. It is often a case of reopening the whole issue and redoing the review. In the case of the water companies, its conclusions are binding, but for gas, electricity and telecoms there is some discretion left to the regulator. He or she, as Howe points out, must balance the needs of the company to finance its business against the interest of the consumers (Howe, 1998, p. 223). The MMC has sustained the RPI$-$X system and made a valuable contribution to consistency in regulatory accounting (Howe, 1998, p. 210).

This type of reference will be largely unaffected by the Competition Act, as will monopoly references under the Fair Trading Act, which still offer the possibility of divestment. There will also be an appeal function. Modelled on EU law, the novel part of the Act for the utilities is the introduction of a prohibition on conduct that may be abuse of a dominant position. Byatt was swift to point out in his 1999 Annual Report that one effect of the Act might be finally to introduce competition into water, since refusing access to company's pipes on reasonable terms might be such an abuse. Price fixing and predatory pricing would also be prohibited. The DGFT and the utility regulators have greater powers to obtain information including the use of 'dawn raids'. They may also borrow staff from each other so specialist OFT investigators can come to the aid of other regulators, who become competition authorities in their own right. For the first time they also possess the power to fine companies. An appeal to the new tribunals set up within the Commission is possible. This holds out the possibility of lighter regulation, but also the potential for appeals from third parties such as consumer groups. Conflicts of interest as always could complicate matters; the duties to promote competition and to protect consumers do not always point in the same direction.

As far as the MMC and the other regulators are concerned, the boundary between policy making and implementation is a key issue. At the outset there was no blueprint for the future development of the utilities. The government had no guidelines to offer the regulators and even at times appeared to let them make policy rather than simply put it into operation. As this chapter has shown, the last two decades have seen a lack of coherence in competition policy. The views of the various regulators have often not been taken into account. The Secretary of State for Trade and Industry has more than once announced the intention to remove decisions on mergers from the political sphere and give them to the competition authorities, paralleling the independence granted to the Bank of England on monetary policy. At the same time ministers intervene, perhaps with greater frequency in issues which are properly the remit of the regulators. The strength of the Competition Commission in this area should be fortified by the provision in the Utilities Act that the recommendation of the Commission on licence amendments should be followed. This represents a reinforcement of accountability. How far parliament can contribute to improved accountability is the subject of the next chapter.

5
The Regulators and Parliament

'I am very conscious of the views of Parliament.'

'What is our accountability? In truth very little…'*

Lack of accountability has been one of the most frequent criticisms levelled at the privatized utilities and those who regulate them (Veljanovski, 1991; Graham, 1995). While it is acknowledged by many that the current situation is an improvement on the days of nationalization, the opinion is widely expressed that the regulators are still insufficiently accountable to the public, to parliament, and to ministers. The situation in the early days was seen by some as shielding executives of the privatized companies from the accountability of ministerial and parliamentary control (Massey, 1993, p. 132). The links between the regulators and the companies and the regulators and the departments were of an informal and, it could be said, secretive character. The discretion which the regulators possessed gave them powers for which they were insufficiently accountable.

As Sir Christopher Foster has pointed out, the doctrine of ministerial responsibility is at its most obscure down among the quangos and non-departmental public bodies. However, ministers retain substantial power and there is an unwritten rule: ministers get their way in the end (Foster, 1994, pp. 270–1).

One object of privatization was to distance operational management from the incessant demands of parliamentary accountability. But as became painfully evident in the case of the nationalized industries, the

---

*Respectively, Stephen Littlechild, TIC, Session 1994–5, HC 481, p. 167; Clare Spottiswoode, quoted in Jenkins, 1996, p. 34.

distinction between operational and policy issues is not a clear-cut one and is never likely to be. It is also evident that the accountability of the regulator or chief executive of an agency to the minister is not the same as the accountability of the minister to parliament. The concept of parliamentary responsibility as expounded by Dicey in the nineteenth century is now of limited use except as a constitutional myth. Following the arms to Iraq affair a nicer distinction exists between 'accountability' meaning providing an answer and 'responsibility' meaning taking the blame (Barberis, 1998, p. 451). An already tricky situation had become trickier as agencies, ombudsmen, and devolution were introduced into the picture. For agencies and other newer adjuncts of government an altered concept of accountability is required. The preceding chapters have shown that in the complex political-economic network under discussion, various checks and balances operate and that transparency is a necessary condition of accountability. Some of that transparency can be provided by Parliament.

There are several specific methods of making regulators accountable. They are answerable to ministers, but also and more importantly to Parliament through an annual report (which is a House of Commons paper) and to the Public Accounts Committee and National Audit Office. Arguably most effective, however, is accountability to select committees. In spite of the fact that power has ebbed away from parliament to the executive and to Europe, the House of Commons (and even occasionally the Lords) can act as the 'Grand Inquest of the Nation' in expressing the concerns and grievances of the people to the government. The select committees, less partisan than other bodies of the House, can fulfil this function better. The committees have the power to summon, in addition to civil servants and ministers, the representative of pressure groups, academics, trade organizations, trade unions, companies and regulatory bodies. They develop an expertise that is an essential contribution to any attempt to analyse and criticize government policy, expose the shortcomings of government agencies or simply raise issues of public importance. Peter Hennessy, while subscribing wholeheartedly to Harold Macmillan's view that 'we have not overthrown the divine right of Kings to fall down before the divine right of experts', rates the new committees established in 1979 as 'the most significant parliamentary development of the post war period' (Hennessy, 1995, pp. 143, 153).

Although they lack the power to initiate policy or scrutinize legislation in advance and their reports are rarely debated in the House, these committees do have influence. The choice of topic to be investigated is theirs, and there is the possibility of 'sustained scrutiny' (Hennessy, 1995, p. 157). Their activities can inconvenience the government. Most ministers, though not obliged to obey the summons, fear the select committees, as do many witnesses. Their reports are anxiously awaited by departments and often smothered and a unanimous report carries weight. But ignoring a report does not kill an issue; there is a valuable tension between the executive and the committee. A select committee report it has been said is more difficult to shrug off than a Royal Commission. The examples that follow include committees returning to issues again and again. They can in this way fulfil the informing function of parliament and provide a forum for debate on proposed reforms, changes in policy and so on, sheltered from the more frenetic atmosphere of the press and broadcasting studios.

The regulators frequently appear before select committees. During the run up to competition in the domestic electricity market, Littlechild gave evidence many times. Clare Spottiswoode faced hostile questioning from several committees. The Trade and Industry Select Committee (TIC), more than any of the others, pursued the issues raised by privatization, though the Employment Committee was intermittently involved and the Energy Select Committee too before its early abolition and absorption into the TIC. Main concerns included the introduction of competition and its effect on customers, and directors' salaries, as well as more general questions about the role of regulators, energy policy and the environment. Littlechild told the committee that he saw his primary accountability as being to Parliament, 'and in practice I think this means this committee or committees like this', and again 'I am very conscious of the views of Parliament' (TIC, Session 1994–5, HC 481, p. 167). Up to now, however, the impact of the select committees on the utilities and their regulation has been mixed. A judgement on their effectiveness would not be especially favourable, as the examples below show. The Liaison Committee, which consists of the chairmen of all the select committees, made an attempt in 2000 to boost their powers. They sought power to scrutinize draft legislation and more time for their reports to be debated on the floor of the House, but this received a negative response from the government.

The decline of the coal industry

Perhaps the most important issue with which the TIC had to deal was the impact of electricity privatization on the coal industry. The industry had been in slow decline ever since the end of the first world war but the effects of the sale of the electricity supply industry were very severe and led to a major political upheaval and recurring crises for successive governments. The crisis that affected the Major government in 1992–3 was dealt with but not resolved, by means of a compromise, a subsidy and ultimately a further reduction in the size of the industry. But the problem of the coal industry was one that would not go away and after the 1997 election the Labour government found itself facing a similar predicament.

The flotation of the two generating companies and the twelve regional electricity companies (RECs) forced into the open complex relationships between electricity, coal and nuclear power. The electricity supply industry had in effect propped up the coal industry for many years, though it in turn was dependent on coal. The history of the mining industry and its relations with governments was a troubled one. Relations between the NUM and the Conservative party had long been characterized by hostility. Outright confrontation had sometimes been avoided, but Edward Heath's showdown with the union in the 1970s had ended in defeat when he called a general election on the issue of 'Who governs Britain?' When Margaret Thatcher became Prime Minister in 1979 she was keen to avenge the humiliation suffered by her party. A keen supporter of nuclear power, she saw it as 'vital to demonstrate to the NUM that coal was not fundamental to the economy any longer' (Young, 1991, p. 168). When shortly after the 1983 election Arthur Scargill, president of the NUM, made a challenging speech promising 'extra-parliamentary action' and the Coal Board announced a programme of redundancies, the scene was set for a strike. Though a national ballot was never held, the dispute was made official in March 1984 and lasted for more than a year. The legacy of bitterness and violence still lingers today in some coal field communities. As a result of the strike and low world energy prices, the industry was decimated; when it finally ended the government was able to justify more closures in the name of an efficient industry. Between 1985 and 1986 and the crisis of 1992, 90,000 miners took voluntary redundancy (Parker, 1993, p. 30).

One effect of the strike had been to delay gas privatization until 1986, but after the 1987 election victory it was possible to contemplate the biggest and most complex privatization of all: electricity. This reform was bound to have an effect on the declining coal industry. British deep mined coal was expensive. Though imports were still small, overseas coal was lower in sulphur as well as lower in cost than British coal. Once in the private sector as National Power and PowerGen, the generators would have greater freedom to choose their source of primary fuel, including cheaper imported coal. This was not the only threat facing the coal industry. The increasing importance of environmental considerations, the availability of natural gas in abundance and the structure and regulation of the privatized electricity industry were all to play a part in its fate. All three factors were to work together against the viability of coal.

Both economic and environmental considerations indicated a bleak future for British coal. This was clearly spelled out by the Energy Select Committee of the House of Commons when it conducted an enquiry into the issue in the winter and spring of 1991. Its report focused mainly on how coal could be cleaned up, but also examined the future of the coal market after 1993, when the contracts agreed at privatization were due to expire (Energy Committee, Session 1992–3, HC 208). With tightening regulations in Europe, acid rain was a growing anxiety. Clean coal technology was being developed, at great expense to the government, but once in the private sector, there would be little interest for the generators in this, and planned new coal plant was abandoned in favour of smaller gas plant. The resulting 'dash for gas' was probably the single most important development in the destruction of the coal industry, prompted by the lifting of the EU ban on the use of gas for electricity generation. The decision permitted investment in a fuel that was attractive not only because it emitted virtually no sulphur and only half the carbon dioxide of coal, but also because of the speed with which power stations could be built. The new technology offered by Combined Cycle Gas Turbines (CCGTs) appealed not only to the small independent power producers (IPPs), which began to be set up once the industry was in the private sector, but also to the large generators faced with installing expensive new cleaning equipment or switching to gas (Green and Newbery, 1997, p. 35). The threat from gas was seen as particularly serious in view of the length of the contracts, commonly fifteen years, but also international coal prices were falling, so imports were likely to rise. Pit closures in practice were virtually irreversible, since mothballing is both expensive and ineffective.

A further report from the committee, published in early 1992, *The Consequences of Electricity Privatization*, criticized the pool, the structure of the ESI and the duopoly. It was realised that the generators would be pressed to short term purchasing decisions, that new entrants into generation would use the new gas technology and that all significant new stations would compete for base load. The implication of this was that the two big generators would almost entirely provide the mid-merit order, that is the variable output, and would thus set the price in the pool.

Powergen and National Power owned all the coal fired stations and were consequently the buyers of the vast bulk of British Coal's production. It was later said that the electricity regulator was in effect also the regulator of the coal industry and there was a good deal of truth in this. Any competition between the two halves of the duopoly would only increase the pressure on British Coal (Parker, 1993, p. 31). Because of the nature of the duopoly, previously parts of the same organization, collusive behaviour was likely, especially since the companies were relatively price insensitive. With a larger number of generators, the switch away from coal might have been slower; five competing ones had been recommended (Green and Newbery, 1997, p. 31). As part of the privatization settlement, a series of contracts had been set up between British Coal and the generating companies, but these lasted only till March 1993, after the next election.

It was a primary duty of the regulator to foster competition and he was keen to encourage entry to the generating sector, which was competitive from the start. The government actively encouraged RECs to develop IPPs. Consent was required for these projects, as it was for such investment by National Power and PowerGen, but neither the DTI, Department of Energy nor the regulator had rejected any projects up to the autumn of 1992. But the market power of NP and PG remained awesome. They had far more capacity than any of their competitors, which was being reduced only slowly, and they generally determined the pool price by using their older coal and oil fired stations (Littlechild, 1995, p. 107).

A serious question here was whether the RECs were purchasing economically. As explained above, they were now allowed to invest in IPPs and as with all generators, this activity was unregulated, as was all electricity generation.[1] Their licences, did, however, include an economic purchasing obligation, which if not adhered to would disallow them from passing on the cost of purchases to the franchise customers. Very complex calculations were involved in this (Newbery and Green, 1996, pp. 66–7), and the power to prevent the pass through of purchase costs to the customer was in the hands of the regulator. This was to become a matter of vital importance: the dash for gas took place with incredible speed. At privatization 92 per cent of fossil fuel generation was coal, only 1 per cent gas (Newbery and Pollitt, 1997, p. 270); by 1996, gas accounted for 23 per cent of generation. The coal industry's decline could only continue.

All of these portents were in the Energy Select Committee's report. But this was its last. As the report was delivered, a general election was in prospect and afterwards the Department of Energy and, as a result, the committee were both abolished. The Conservative government, returned with a small majority, had by autumn 1992 not found a solution to the problem of the pit closures that were bound to take place when the 1990 contracts ended. So, when the coal crisis erupted, responsibility for the matters previously dealt with by the department were split. The supply side functions were now dealt with by the DTI and energy efficiency and environmental and planning issues including combined heat and power (CHP), by the Department of the Environment – a division that was to continue and would be the source of problems. The DTI was pressing the generators to take extra coal, which they were reluctant to do, because the pass through of coal costs by the RECs might not be allowed. The planned sell off of the coal industry would be jeopardized if there were no agreement.

When in October 1992 Michael Heseltine, then President of the Board of Trade, announced to the House of Commons that the majority of Britain's 50 remaining deep mines would close, there was a public outcry almost without precedent. People who had no connection with mining districts demonstrated in protest, even in areas that might be expected to be loyal to the Conservative party. Many seemed to agree with Arthur Scargill's pronouncement that it was a 'deliberate political act of industrial vandalism' (*Times*, 14 Oct. 1992).

But it was the strength of opposition on the government backbenches that really prompted the government's climb down a few days later. Marcus Fox, Chairman of the 1922 Committee, told the government that a review of the decision was 'imperative'. Winston Churchill said 'If you're going up a blind alley, the most sensible thing to do is to make a U-turn' (*Times*, 17 Oct. 1992). And so it was. The government announced that only ten of the 31 threatened collieries would close and final decisions would be taken on the rest in the New Year. The terms of the review included an individual examination of each mine plus a review of the consent powers for new CCGT plant.

The house also voted for an enquiry by the Select Committee on Trade and Industry. The DTI and the committee were in some senses working together: seeking a means to increase the market for coal. Measures being considered included subsidies, a levy on electricity consumers or legislation to encourage consumers to burn more coal. (*Times*, 10 Dec. 1992). However, confusion and lack of communication within and between the government and British Coal were apparent.

The committee's main aim, like that of the DTI review, published at the eleventh hour in March 1993 under the title *The Prospects for Coal*, was to see if a way could be found to enlarge the market for coal. Taking an immense amount of evidence from a huge range of witnesses, the committee reviewed all the alternative fuel sources from imported coal to orimulsion, taking into account security of supply, environmental considerations and cost, without really coming up with any feasible suggestions for cutting back on any of them. The main proposal was that the generators should receive a subsidy up to 1998 to enable them to burn more British coal. It also recommended that the Nuclear Review, due in 1994, should be brought forward by one year. The government agreed to these proposals, though the subsidy was 'vague and temporary' (Parker and Surrey, 1993, p. 399). A reconsideration of the Fossil Fuel Levy was also agreed on, as well as the setting up of an Energy Advisory Panel, but a planned energy policy was firmly rejected.

In addition the government would not accept some of the other main recommendations, including the postponement of the reduction in the RECs' franchise in 1994 to 1998, which would have made it easier to agree contracts for more coal. The DTI report insisted that the first stage of competition in electricity supply should go ahead as set out in the Electricity Act. This was a strong reason for the RECs' reluctance to commit themselves to long term contracts.

Littlechild, under mounting pressure, had made an announcement of his own late in 1992: that he would bring forward his review of the RECs' purchasing policies. He had said that he would not vet in advance the contracts they signed with the IPPs, he was only interested in a 'reasonable balance' in a portfolio (*Times*, 19 Oct. 1992). Furthermore, he denied any responsibility for wider matters of national energy policy, such as the fate of the coal industry: a view that he continued to hold over the next five years.

When it came to the committee hearing, Littlechild argued that he could not scrutinize every contract. He ultimately exonerated the RECs in two separate reports, but the Committee was not satisfied with this and expressed the judgement that he was late, superficial and ignored the coal alternative. It also felt that he took a narrow view of consumer interests, seeing the issue as primarily one of introducing competition. So the committee wanted the Secretary of State to be able to require the DGES (the regulator) to make a review, and also felt strongly that protection of consumers should be a primary duty. It was to take a new government and new legislation to make progress on this.

When the DTI report *The Prospects for Coal* appeared in March 1993, like many such responses it was rather short and conceded only a small part of what the committee had recommended. Competition therefore won the day. Even the proposal to alter arrangements for planning new generating capacity was turned down: a planned energy policy was firmly rejected. There was to be no moderation of the dash for gas; as Parker and Surrey note 'within two months of the publication of *The Prospects for Coal*, a further planned 3 gigawatts (GW) of CCGT plant had been given the go-ahead' (Parker and Surrey, 1993, p. 399). The committee also made two recommendations on the powers of the regulator: that he should have greater power over the generators' prices and that he should take into account the 'legitimate interests of indigenous fuel producers' (Parker and Surrey, 1993, p. 399). Neither of these was accepted at the time but the generators' prices were to be capped in 1994, and the question of the interests of the coal industry was to resurface in 1997. The commitment to privatize the coal industry was also reaffirmed.

This episode coincided with many other troubles for the government – party divisions over the Maastricht treaty, rising unemployment, the forced devaluation of the pound and the failure of the attempt to join the ERM – partly succeeding in putting off the issue of what would happen to the coal industry after March 1993, but completely misjudging the public reaction to the contraction in the coal market. After the brief moratorium on pit closures, however, and when a temporary subsidy had been put in place, it stuck to its market policy and left the coal industry to its fate. Though it was the electricity industry that was privatized, it was the coal industry that was exposed to the chill winds of competition. As for the regulator, he stuck to his chief objective, the introduction of greater competition. He permitted the cost pass-through for the RECs but only at the price of adhering to the programme for the introduction of competition to the electricity supply industry – 'a masterly political manoeuvre' according to one commentator (Helm, 1993, p. 100). In pursuit of competition, he was also considering forcing the generators to sell some of their coal fired capacity. This he did, and the sale eventually took place – to Eastern Group, the largest REC, and this was to be the first step towards the reintegration of generation and supply which had been separated at privatization. Thus some hard choices were put off until after the 1997 general election. Nothing was done to increase the market for coal and as 1998 approached more contraction in the industry seemed likely as coal contracts once again came to an end.

The debate continued on how far a regulator should become involved in wider policy issues. So did the death throes of the British coal industry, but once privatized, the government's attempts to influence both electricity and coal producers were even more problematic. When British Coal was sold off in 1994, the bulk of the assets were bought by RJB mining. Formerly a purely open cast operation, floated on the stock market in June 1993, RJB had got off to a flying start with the large, profitable take or pay five-year contracts negotiated with National Power and PowerGen by the government to ensure a successful sale. At the end of 1996, the company started trying to renegotiate these; but the outlook for British coal had deteriorated and room for manoeuvre was limited.

The strength of sterling made imported coal cheaper and the proximity of 1998 and competition in the electricity market also put pressure on prices. In opposition Labour had criticized the encouragement given to the 'dash for gas'; once in office they approved several new CCGT plants. Each new gas fired station reduced the overall demand for coal. Nuclear power stations, previously thought to be on the point of decommissioning, were being used for longer. Environmental pressures were also increasing. The high chlorine content of much of RJB's coal meant it had to be mixed with open cast or imported coal, both of which were cheaper. Thus, though there was strong opposition to open cast mining, there were also fears that if it was restricted, more deep mining jobs might be lost. By autumn 1997 all of these factors meant the possibility of large-scale redundancies, and as a result there was something like a re-run, though on a smaller scale, of the events of the autumn of 1992, but with a changed cast of characters, whose political priorities were rather different. Richard Budge, head of RJB, whose management style was chiefly characterized by brinkmanship, was to become a thorn in the side of the government.

Initially the government refused to get involved. Budge had done very well out of the privatization of British Coal and there were several reasons to ignore his pleas for help. The Kyoto conference was approaching and aid to the coal industry would cut across the commitment made to cut carbon dioxide emissions by 20 per cent from 1990 levels by 2010. The series of reviews set up by the government had still to report and this undoubtedly aggravated the tendency to delay. The government was still enjoying its post election honeymoon and no minister had a coal field constituency. But it was not to last.

As five years previously the government was impelled to action by pressure from the backbenches when the House resumed after the long summer recess, following an adjournment debate initiated by Conservative MP Bill Cash. He called for the extension of the coal contracts for a further two years and accused the government of 'betraying their heritage', adding 'new Labour is killing the coal industry' (Hansard, Commons, Session 1997–8, vol. 29, cols 1000–1008).

The cabinet decided on a review of the coal industry, which was to be conducted by Richard Caborn, who had been chairman of the committee in 1992 and was now a minister at the DETR. It was decided that some support might be forthcoming from the government after Budge had reached agreement with the generators. The Industry Minister, John Battle, was summoned to appear before the Trade and Industry Committee in early December. Battle, it was widely known, opposed restrictions on new gas fired plants, indeed he had been under attack for having breached Labour's 1992 pledge not to licence any (*Times*, 26 June 1998). His evidence to the Committee had vehemently stated that such a move would serve no purpose. He argued that it would take three or four years for new gas stations to be commissioned, so there would be no benefit to the coal industry before 2000. Restricting consents would also slow down the progress of CHP projects. Applications would be carefully considered, not waved through (TIC, Session 1997–8, HC 404, para. 39). Amid mounting tension however, and immediately before Battle was to face the committee, Blair announced during Prime Minister's Questions a moratorium on the building of more CCGT power stations, 'pending a review of long term energy requirements'. Blair's statement made clear to what extent the minister had been sidelined. Battle arrived to give evidence to find that the prime minister had just delivered his statement.

However, it was a measure of how opinion had shifted since the industry had been moved into the private sector that this question could be asked of the Prime Minister by a South Yorkshire MP:

> Does my Right Hon friend agree that, in view of the fact that RJB Mining made profits of £173 m in 1995, and £189 m last year, questions about the future of the coal mines that Mr Budge owns should be addressed, first and foremost to Mr Budge?'
>
> (Hansard, Commons, Session 1997–8, vol. 302, col. 348)

A week after the announcement of the moratorium, the prime minister once again at question time told the House that an agreement had been reached which offered the mining company a six-month delay. This was rather more than the truth but it represented a temporary fix that provided a three-month breathing space. This was a battle between New and old Labour. The latter had had much of its credibility restored by the success of the revolt over one parent benefit (*Economist*, 13 Dec. 1997), the government's other major headache at the time.

It was clear that the generators might exact a heavy price for making concessions to Budge. Powergen, it was widely known, was keen to purchase a REC, having been denied one by Ian Lang in 1995. Eastern wanted to convert two of its stations to burn gas as well as coal, but it had a five-year agreement with RJB and so an end to the moratorium would pacify it. National Power would be harder to please. The government spent many hours trying to broker a deal. The aim now was to 'level the playing field' for coal. Quite how this was to be done remained unclear, but Littlechild's enquiry into the operation of the electricity pool, set up in October, included the phrase 'avoiding discrimination against particular energy sources' in its terms of reference. The regulator himself made his view clear: safeguarding the coal industry was not a sensible course of action (*Times*, 9 April 1998).

The government considered various possibilities to improve the market for coal. These included the idea of selling coal to Germany and Spain, the further sale of generating capacity by the two large generators, accelerated installation of FGD equipment and reducing French electricity imports through the interconnector. None of these offered any realistic prospects of enlarging British coal sales, but they strongly resembled the remedies suggested by the select committee five years earlier when Caborn, now a minister at the DETR, had been chairman of the Trade and Industry Committee. The difficulty of achieving this seemed even greater when the Environment Agency announced that it would bring forward stricter controls on sulphur dioxide emissions.

The select committee's report appeared in April 1998 (HC 404, *Coal*). By this time Budge had reached agreement with the Energy Group and National Power but was still pressing the government for more. The report was severely critical of Budge; the committee took the view that he was the author of his own downfall. More surprisingly perhaps, the report was cool on the subject of propping up the moribund coal industry. In a second report on *Energy Policy* that swiftly followed that on coal, the committee concluded: 'So long as gas remains cheaper than coal and cleaner and more efficient, there are no good reasons to obstruct its wider use. Nor are there any environmental grounds for protecting coal' (TIC, Session 1997–8, HC 471, para. 42).

There was a short-lived rearguard action mounted by Lord Ezra, former NCB chairman and member of the 1945 Attlee government.

This took the form of a private bill that aimed to extend the uses to which the Fossil Fuel Levy could be put, in particular to use it to support clean coal technology and CHP schemes. But the government moved against it at the second reading and killed it off (Hansard, Lords, Session 1997–8, vol. 587, col. 413). Within the government, disagreement continued on whether intervention on behalf of coal was appropriate or not. The moratorium idea persisted, though the CBI had come out firmly against it along with the gas companies and the environmental lobby. The problem facing the government was much the same as in 1993, trying to save the coal industry by persuading the big generators to commit themselves to contracts at figures above market prices. But there was also a commitment to increase competition in the electricity market generally and this deal, should it be concluded, would result in less rather than more competition, continuing a situation in which the three coal generators set the price about 85 per cent of the time. Essentially then, this was the same dilemma as in 1993. If more competition really did develop in the generation market, the argument against vertical integration would lose its force.

The possibility of a reference to the MMC on the question of power station sales, though they had been assured that no more would be required, was floated by Littlechild, who was concerned that any measures which the government thought it right to introduce to protect coal should not have a negative impact on competition or customers in the electricity industry. He admitted, however, that 'It's a matter for the government and not myself to worry about the future of the British coal industry' (*Times*, 18 June 1998). As in 1993, he favoured increasing competition and this time found himself more in agreement with the select committee: 'Gas fired investment is a rational response to environmental constraints and economic realities' (*Financial Times*, 7 Aug. 1998).

The result of the pool review brought no joy to the generators either: Littlechild's report recommended a three-tier market with demand side bidding and futures contracts; but it seemed unlikely to reduce the price setting powers of the generators. In late June the conclusions of the government's energy review were published, only 48 hours before the expiry of the extended coal contracts. No deals had yet been announced, no guaranteed tonnages as Budge had wanted, but the gas moratorium was effectively extended by two years and the big generators would be forced to dispose of plant as well as agree to changes to the electricity trading arrangements. The review dealt coal a blow however by dropping any new commitment to clean coal technology. Margaret Beckett, President of the Board of Trade and clearly identified with old Labour, insisted that environmental targets would be met and then left the series of conflicting interests, interlocking policy issues and difficult choices, including that of the new energy regulator and the final decision on the moratorium, to be dealt with by her successor, Peter Mandelson.

Perhaps the trickiest of these was the question of power station disposals that became, not unexpectedly, intertwined with the PowerGen takeover of East Midlands Electricity announced in July 1998. The deal was cleared when Powergen agreed to divest 4 GW of capacity, as described in the previous chapter. The regulator, however, would have liked 6 GW and a total of 10 GW by the two biggest generators (*Financial Times*, 7 Aug. 1998). Mandelson preferred these demands to be scaled down so that an MMC reference could be avoided. By October, Budge had signed contracts with National Power, but PowerGen and Eastern were still holding back and the White Paper on energy sources, the last of the reviews, was published. This confirmed the moratorium that Mandelson described as 'short term and temporary' (*Independent*, 9 Oct. 1998), but which would continue until the regulator advised him that competition was sufficiently established. There was no target for what proportion of electricity should be generated from coal, but a clear hope or expectation that new contracts would be signed. This was inseparable from the issue of divestment to be negotiated with the regulator. The government did not argue a special case for coal, rather that the electricity market was suffering from distortions; a level playing field was what was needed. NETA was supposed to provide this. So as in 1993, the compromise such as it was, was presented as consistent with competition (Helm, 1998c).

The agreements which were finally arrived at in 1998, though they enabled RJB to keep going without closing pits, and allowed the government to shelve the question until after the next election (Edwards, 1999), did nothing to stop the decline in coal burn from 1999 on. The select committee's second report on *Energy Policy* in the summer of 1998 had been very critical of the government letting so much time pass before initiating a review. At the same time they were at a loss to understand why the review was necessary, since the UK has an unusually diverse mix of energy resources. They therefore did not favour the moratorium and implored the government to move to better co-ordination of energy and environmental policies (TIC, Session 1997–8, HC 471, para. 32).

Mandelson said, 'I am not passing down a God-given right to Mr Budge to produce coal which others will buy' (*Guardian*, 9 Oct. 1998).

Indeed RJB was struggling to the point of seeking government aid early in 2000. The Secretary of State, Byers, under twin pressures, from RJB to help keep the coal industry afloat and from gas and electricity producers to remove the moratorium, gave in to both. Diversity was a possible justification for propping up an industry that faced a bleak future even when prices were rising. After some delay, possibly a result of civil service opposition to a subsidy that it was feared might be vetoed by the EU competition authorities, a £100 million package was announced in April 2000. It was to be spread over two to three years, that is until the next election was out of the way, and would be used to reduce the price paid by the new American owners of Drax, Europe's largest coal-fired power station. The restricted consent policy for new gas-fired plant was lifted in late 2000, but the new electricity trading arrangements were postponed until 2001. Trying to control the market power of the generators, reduce prices to consumers and not close down the British coal industry constituted a political and economic balancing act unforeseen at the time of electricity privatization, even without the renewed pressure on environmental pollution.

These two separate crises have a good deal in common and some interesting differences. Both came at a bad time for the government. In the first case, the government's majority was small and the pound had just been forced humiliatingly out of the ERM. In the second the Labour government was facing its first serious problem in the shape of a back bench rebellion, backed by considerable public feeling, on the issue of benefits for single parents. In 1992, the employment implications of mining redundancies were large. By 1997, there were more people employed in call centres than in mining and the environmental aspects loomed much larger. The Conservatives set themselves against supporting the coal industry and leaving it to market forces but fixed contracts to last till 1998, so that the industry could be sold off. In 1997 as in 1992 there was considerable reluctance to intervene in an industry that it was by now in the private sector, but the government put in place the stricter consents policy which was in direct opposition to its environmental commitments and was widely deplored. In both cases the market power of the generators was blamed, but the Labour government's solution did nothing to reduce that, rather the reverse. In 1993 the electricity regulator was something of a scapegoat but in 1998 he and the select committee shared the view that the coal industry should not be artificially preserved.

The committee's chief contribution in both cases was to provide a forum for discussion of the issues; its influence on the outcome was not significant.

The Employment Select Committee

In the 1993 coal crisis, one select committee enquiry was not enough for the Commons. A second, this time by the Employment Committee, was also started. Its scope was as large and its list of witnesses equally impressive. There was also a huge range of written evidence, from people as diverse as Arthur Scargill and the Bishop of Lichfield. At the eleventh hour – immediately after Heseltine's announcement – Peter Walker, a former cabinet minister, was brought in to lead efforts to regenerate the coal mining districts. Up to 30,000 jobs were at stake, and the knock on effects in the rail industry in particular were expected to be serious. The committee's report revealed a total lack of information and consultation; little preparation had taken place. No calculations had been done on the social and other costs of so large a number of redundancies concentrated in particular areas. Nor had the two secretaries of state, for industry and employment, had a meeting on the issue. The chairman of the coal board had not succeeded in obtaining an interview with the secretary of state for employment in the summer. The President of the Board of Trade (Michael Heseltine) had completely misjudged the extent to which public opinion could be prepared for an event of this kind by leaks from the Rothschild committee, which in 1991 had foreseen a future with as few as a dozen pits. This report was never published, but there had been reports in the press all through the year indicating that widespread pit closures were likely to be necessary if the industry was to be sold off, a long-term commitment of the Conservative government. In spite of the public indignation, it seemed in the end that the bitter remark made by the leader of the UDM to the Employment Select Committee had a good deal of truth in it: 'I believe … one at a time they will be knocked off and there will not be a public outcry' (Employment Committee, Session 1992–3, HC 263, Evidence, Q147).

Influential they may have been but in both of these cases the impact of the select committees was very limited.

Salaries of chief executives of utilities

In 1995, the Employment Select Committee also investigated the hotly debated question of the salaries and perks awarded to the directors and chief executives of the privatized utilities in the summer of 1995 when it was constantly in the news, with British Gas the chief quarry. The public perception, encouraged by the press, was that utilities were not as other companies even though they were no longer publicly-owned but now had shareholders. At that stage most were monopolies or near-monopolies and still run by many of the same people who had run them before privatization. The prime minister, having previously stated that executive pay was a matter for shareholders, then changed his opinion and described the increases as 'distasteful' (Hansard, Commons, 28 Feb. 1995, vol. 255, col. 837). It was apparently at his behest that the Greenbury Committee was set up by the CBI. This was a matter of great public controversy. The Select Committee called as witnesses Cedric Brown (twice), Gordon Brown, who joined the chorus of disapproval, Iain Vallance and Clare Spottiswoode. Cedric Brown, who had been the focus of particular vilification in the press, admitted to having been 'tactless and insensitive' over his large salary increase when staff in gas showrooms were being fired and service standards were slipping (Employment Committee, 1995–6, HC 159, para. 1). The information gathered for the report, however, revealed that though the directors of the utilities had benefited from large percentage increases, other large companies such as Mobil, Barclays and ICI paid their chief executives far more. The members of the Greenbury committee mostly received far larger sums than any senior executive with a utility. Sir Richard Greenbury received over £1 million (para. 40), and Sir Iain Vallance of BT, also a member of that committee, was earning over £600,000 and himself displayed a lack of tact and sensitivity when he told the committee that the job of a junior hospital doctor might be more relaxing than his own (para. 43). There was not much evidence that these increases were justified by performance, as the press did not fail to point out (*Times*, 31 May 1995). The committee recalled Cedric Brown when it became known that he had failed to disclose details of a new long-term incentive scheme. Sir Richard Greenbury himself insisted on speaking to the committee in private, when he apparently told MPs that the utility pay rises were 'disgraceful' (*Times*, 19 April 1995).

The whole affair had the air of a show trial, and the controversy over Brown's salary became entangled with the cash for questions controversy and the hints of political corruption which hung over the last two years of the Major government. British Gas may have been the target of some unfair criticism, but the company's reputation was not enhanced by the news that Giordano was saving tax by having half of his half million pound salary paid in dollars (*Economist*, 24 Feb. 1996).

In general those who gave evidence took the view that regulators should not be involved in questions of executive pay, that this was a job for shareholders. Clare Spottiswoode told the committee that any change would be a question for Parliament, but pointed out that it was odd to treat British Gas differently from other companies. The salary of the chief executive did not affect the price of gas. If a comparison was made between the salary and the gas bill, a 28 per cent increase for Brown would cost each customer only half a penny a year, so it was a very small part of the costs considered by the regulator when setting prices. She said that she saw her job as very apolitical and if regulators became involved in decisions about salaries they would have undue influence over companies.

This enquiry lasted a long time, and heard a great deal of evidence, as indeed did the Greenbury committee. Unlike most select committee reports, there was a deep division on party lines and the committee failed to come up with any clear recommendations. It did little more than set out the arguments on both sides – whether the directors in question were doing much the same job as before and the nature and extent of their responsibilities. Following the Cadbury committee that had reported on corporate governance in 1992, the committee recommended that institutional shareholders should play a greater part, and that executive share options should never be issued at a discount, but appeared to be satisfied that these issues were being dealt with. The need for 'sensitivity' in handling salary increases was also mentioned. Greater disclosure was widely agreed to be the best means of controlling excessive pay outs, but as with salary levels, utilities were revealed to be more open than other companies. Accountability to shareholders should be improved but there was no recommendation for enforced regulation of pay levels. The Greenbury Committee itself faced similar differences of opinion among its members with similarly anodyne results.

The Public Accounts Committee, by contrast, studying the work of the regulators at about the same time was prepared to be much more emphatic, expressing the view that public confidence might be damaged, especially since job losses in the privatized companies and falling service standards were occurring simultaneously. It recommended that the directors general should use their influence on executive pay levels (PAC, Session 1995–6, HC 159, para. 77). The Employment Committee's report stated that it was intended to inform public debate, but its failure to do more than this showed how the select committees depend for their effect on a cross-party approach.

The Labour Party reaped a handsome dividend from this controversy. It provided the inspiration for the windfall tax, which while not hurting consumers managed at once to hit the hated utility companies and to bring huge sums into the Treasury for a good cause, the 'New Deal' for the young unemployed. Once in government Labour attempted to put pressure on directors about salary increases, but to little effect. Intervention was difficult, since there was no breach of the city codes devised successively by Cadbury, Greenbury and Hampel. However, the new legislation in 2000 included a provision for regulators to link salaries to customer service standards.

The liberalization of the electricity industry

Unlike the liberalization of the low volume gas market, bringing competition into electricity supply was provided for in the original legislation. This was to take place in three stages, starting in 1990 with the market for approximately 5,000 very large customers, with a peak demand of 1 MW or more. Secondly in 1994 came buyers of more than 100 kW. Finally in 1998 the RECs would lose their regional franchises and the rest of the market, more than 25 million domestic customers and small businesses, would be able to choose their supplier. There was therefore eight years' notice for OFFER and the RECs to organize a very large and complex system. The first two moves to liberalization had not gone smoothly; overall responsibility for the project had not been taken by anyone. There had been delays in installing metering equipment and failures in communication systems, as well as a lack of adequate trials. The management consultants Coopers and Lybrand, who had been retained, foresaw a potential disaster (TIC, Session 1995–6, HC 481, para. 21). Gas, less complex than electricity, had had plenty of problems during the 'rollout' of competition. The liberalization of gas had prompted a serious examination of social concerns, such as fuel poverty. This in turn influenced the committee's views on electricity liberalization and it pressed the regulator on such issues as switching supplier with debt and prepayment metering.

As a result of these anxieties, the Trade and Industry Committee conducted an enquiry, in 1995 (*Aspects of the ESI*, Session 1995–6, HC 481), which found that there was serious cause for concern about those preparations. The committee decided to investigate four aspects: what the costs and benefits of the project were, whether the benefits would extend to all customers, whether responsibility for the whole operation had been allocated and whether the extension of competition on such a large scale was practicable. Three years later, in spite of valiant efforts by the committee, the answers to these questions remained unclear.

At this time, the spring and summer of 1995, the whole electricity industry was in turmoil as a result of the decision of the regulator to reopen his distribution price review. Furthermore, the generating companies that had started out after privatization quite unregulated had

had price caps imposed after the coal crisis and were now supposed to be divesting some of their plant to improve competition in generation. Takeover activity was also beginning in the sector, as the golden shares expired. So the system as set up in 1989–91 was undergoing quite considerable change and was affected by a great deal of uncertainty. The committee recommended a cost–benefit analysis, the regulation of prices and standards for a certain period, a central co-ordinator or project manager, a timetable and trials, as in gas. When examined, the electricity regulator rejected the term 'chaos' for the 1994 reduction in the franchise, but admitted that there were lessons to be learned. He did not want to assume extra powers for himself, but agreed to take on the role of co-ordinator (TIC, Session 1994–5, HC 481, para. 23).

Apart from the organization of the project, the committee also focused on its likely impact on smaller consumers. The larger customers in the remaining franchise were very likely to benefit, but those who used small amounts of power were not. The margins were thin and there was less chance than in gas of significant cross-subsidies being uncovered, since there were no stranded contracts to hamper the incumbent and encourage entry. A chief concern of the committee was that the incumbent RECs might be left with a disproportionate number of those requiring special services, the rest being 'cherry picked' by new entrants (TIC, Session 1994–5, HC 481, para. 15). To the regulator, equal social obligations for all suppliers was desirable 'eventually'; the committee thought it should happen from the start.

The committee returned to the subject in 1996 (report *Liberalisation of the Electricity Market*, HC 279, published March 1997) to find out what progress had been made and to see what lessons could be learned from the experience of liberalization of the gas market. By this time, PA Consulting, which had been appointed overall programme manager (OPM), had prevailed on the regulator to agree to a phased approach. This would be based on post codes and would mean that only ten per cent of customers would have the opportunity to choose their electricity supplier from 1 April 1998. Questioned by the committee, Littlechild denied that he could have overall control of 14 companies. He told the Public Accounts Committee that it was now 'a very large logistical problem' (PAC, Session 1996–7, HC 89, para. 11). All he could do was co-ordinate. The DTI, however, took the view that Littlechild did have the overall responsibility.

OFFER had begun to take a more central role, but some felt that there was still not enough central authority and that this was exacerbated by the fragmented structure of the industry. Trials were still not planned and some PESs thought they would cause further delays. On the question of costs, by this time estimated at £1 billion, and whether such an upheaval would be worthwhile, Littlechild remained optimistic. The cost–benefit analysis commissioned by OFFER estimated that benefits could total six to eight times that. Achievability it seemed was mostly dependent on information systems being ready. The committee took the view that postponement was not yet justified but clearly a possibility and that contingency plans were needed. There was a tremendous amount of work to do on designing IT systems, drawing up legal agreements, codes and licences. Numerous committees sprang up and there were employment opportunities for many management consultants and former utility workers (Westlake, 1997, p. 25). There were disagreements on whether customers in debt would be allowed to switch supplier and on disconnection for non-payment.

By the time that the Labour government was elected in May 1997 it was clear that the committee's fears were well founded. Software problems in the pool were threatening a delay to the planned start date of 1 April 1998. It had already been decided to phase in the change, but as delays and costs mounted there were suspicions that some RECs had been dragging their feet, mistakenly anticipating a deferral if Labour won (*Financial Times*, 2 June 1997; TIC, Session 1994–5, HC 481, para. 48). This misapprehension was dispelled when John Battle, now the industry minister, took personal responsibility for completing the project, stressing that it must 'benefit the many, not the few'. Fuel poverty was already an important item on the government's agenda (*Financial Times*, 5 June 1997). The regulator blamed the delays on computer problems, but the IT people said they were due to lack of direction. In spite of Battle's efforts, the timetable continued to slip and in early 1998 – with the delay said to be 'purely technical', the start was put off till the following September, with the roll out stretching into early summer of the following year. The DGES accepted the decision of the OPM, but retained the possibility of opening earlier in some areas if progress permitted. Since the introduction of competition to the gas industry was virtually complete, electricity companies had an opportunity to enter these markets when their own were still closed; a cause of major irritation to Centrica, the only company ready to sell electricity nationwide.

The Trade and Industry Committee had clearly decided to pursue this to the bitter end. Its final report on the matter came out in July 1998. While approving the decision to postpone, it laid the blame, especially for starting so late, on the lack of a project manager before

September 1995. It recognized that not all the RECs were committed to the opening up of the market, but criticized the lack of a central authority. Documentation had been inadequate and testing delayed. In particular it was severely critical of the huge cost overrun: as one writer commented, the 1998 project assumed a life not dissimilar to a black hole – 'where resources were digested with consummate ease without any apparent effect on the appetite for more' (Westlake, 1997, p. 21). Though the committee's previous reports had pressured the electricity regulator and the PA manager to improve organization, the incentives to the PESs had not been sufficient to speed up their preparations. They were about to lose their monopolies and the fines levied on those which fell behind were inadequate. The committee stuck to its terms of reference as set out in 1995, which included the social agenda and the need for responsibility to be taken in organizing what was the largest IT project in the world.

The regulator paid tribute to the contribution of the DTI once the new government had come in. The committee grilled him once again on escalating costs and the problems of doorstep selling. He promised consumers would be provided with adequate information to enable them to make informed choices. He also foresaw the merging of supply businesses, something in which London Electricity and Eastern led the way in 1999.

This is an example of a select committee doing its duty by exposing 'a sorry story' (TIC, Session 1997–8, 10th Report, *Developments in the Liberalisation of the Electricity Market*, HC 871), and in the earlier stages looking at something which was perhaps being neglected by the government. Its reports detailed the inadequacy of the performance of OFFER and the management consultant which was running the project, eliciting facts and forecasts and in particular the huge amount it all cost, which was to be added to customers' bills. The regulator was being accountable – he was cross examined by the committee on at least three occasions over this and commented that he saw his primary accountability as being to parliament. He was always unruffled, but reluctant to take full responsibility.

'Joined up government' notwithstanding, select committees can also perform a useful role in pointing out the conflicting objectives adopted by the government. One example is the TIC's report on the climate change levy (CCL), which pointed out that government policy on energy use is pulling in a different direction to the commitment of the DTI and the regulator to reduce energy prices (TIC, Session 1998–9, HC 678, para. 21). This is also true of the twin aims to protect the coal industry and the need to cut back carbon dioxide emissions. The government's response to the report refused to acknowledge this.

One idea that has gained a wide measure of support is that of a specific select committee to cover the utilities; it could be a permanent sub-committee of the Trade and Industry Committee. Some regulators and some politicians favoured this innovation, along with academics and regulated companies. It was not however welcomed by the TIC itself. It would cut across existing departmental committees and might duplicate their work. Questions would arise about precisely which industries should be included. Railways, for instance, might be, but the rail regulator would also choose to be in the remit of the transport committee. Such a change might therefore undermine the system of select committees and, in the committee's view, would not actually increase accountability. The basis of the system is that select committees shadow departments and this is the root of the antagonism to the idea of a committee dedicated to the utilities.

The Environmental Audit Committee, set up in November 1997, was not a select committee and indeed its existence rather emphasised the fact that environmental issues were generally being treated as an 'add-on'. It did, however, do valuable work in highlighting the divergence of views between the environment minister (DETR) and the energy minister (DTI). This was made very clear when during the enquiry into energy efficiency, the environment minister said that the moratorium on consents for gas-fired power stations 'was designed to help the hard hit coal industry'. The industry minister disagreed with this: 'it is nothing to do with the coal industry. The coal industry digs the coal out.' But he went on to say: 'in a sense it will work through to ensure that coal-burning power stations get a look in. To that extent I may simply be playing with words' (*Environmental Audit Committee*, Session 1998–9, HC 159, para. 32).

It is not surprising therefore that the committee saw the stricter consents policy as 'serving no particular purpose'. It was part of the new government's attempts to ensure that the idea of sustainable development was 'not a bolt-on extra but informs the whole of government' (*Environmental Audit Committee*, Session 1998–9, HC 246, para. 3). The problems they faced in doing so are dealt with in the next chapter.

6
The Impact of Environmental Policies

'Environmental improvements are not a free lunch.'*

Introduction

As has already been made clear, utility companies, a vital part of the economic infrastructure of the country, have an important impact on environmental issues. They are big users of primary resources – gas, coal, water, and so on. They are also big polluters. Energy is fundamental to all economic activity and the burning of coal, gas and oil for electricity generation gives rise to considerable pollution in the form of greenhouse gases, acid rain and poor air quality which has implications for human health as well as the natural environment. Water is essential both for domestic and industrial life and water quality requires careful monitoring. Since environmental costs are often externalities, that is they are not included in the market prices of goods and services, the price of the good does not reflect its true cost to society. Consequently these costs are also often an afterthought when policies are being formed. To take account of such externalities or internalise them, it is necessary to assign them a value or price, not an easy task, and one not always popular with environmentalists (Stirling, 1992).

This is a very broad subject with much scientific and technical content. In this chapter it will only be possible to outline the complexities of integrating environmental with economic and social policies and the implications of that both for the regulators and government.

The major international environmental problems of greenhouse gases and air pollution can be seen as a special sort of externality; sometimes

*Ian Byatt, Director of Water Services, 1998.

referred to as the 'tragedy of the commons'. A 'commons' is a resource that is owned by no one but which each has a right to use. The effect of each person pursuing their own individual interests is the destruction of the asset held in common. In the same way, the damage done by greenhouse gases will affect all. It is therefore not rational for states to act alone on such matters. This provides the best possible case for international co-operation (see Beckerman, 1996). The fact that so many pollution issues are international in nature and therefore involve much larger political communities, only serves to make solutions even harder to reach. Holes in the ozone layer, loss of bio-diversity and other environmental problems are also by their nature in general long-term issues and as a result, competing short-term political pressures often take precedence.

The UK amongst other nations signed the first international environmental agreement with definite targets, the Montreal Protocol on CFC gases, in 1987. The UK government had a mediocre record in environmental protection. The following year, the prime minister, Margaret Thatcher, made a speech to the Royal Society in which she stressed the importance of developing policy to deal with climate change (*Times*, 28 Sep. 1988). By the time of the Earth Summit in Rio in 1992, environmental awareness had become much more widespread and the government had made a commitment to establish an Environment Agency.

UK environmental policy is ostensibly based on the notion of sustainability. A White Paper of 1990, *This Common Inheritance*, set out the government's view of what the concept entailed and acknowledged the international scope of environmental problems but any precision the concept may once have had has long since been eroded (Helm, 1998a). During the period of Conservative government, economic growth was included in the definition and Labour more recently added social considerations. These accretions make the meaning of sustainability much broader, some might argue almost meaningless; but the concept, however defined, is a long term one, which implies not mortgaging the future and safeguarding our children's inheritance. It also implies an alteration in human behaviour, so that decisions are taken with regard to their environmental impact. Trade-offs are thus essential and this is the crux of the matter, and the source of many political difficulties.

Lord Wakeham, then Energy Secretary, provided an example of the low priority given to environmental considerations in 1992. Spelling out the government's energy policy, he spoke of the importance of promoting competition, of keeping energy prices low, of preserving diversity of supply and so on, coming only at the end to 'meeting the growing requirements of environmental policy' (Hansard, Lords, vol. 539, cols 669–70).

Since the late 1980s when climate change and global warming became a preoccupation, government statements have had a ring of all things to all people about them. For example the 1998 White Paper on Energy Sources for Power Generation declared: 'Sustainable development is about ensuring a better quality of life for everyone now and for generations to come' (DTI, 1998, p. 69).

At the beginning of the new century, this is just as much the case as a decade earlier under the Conservative government. There is a good deal to support the suspicion that politicians of both main parties are only paying lip service to the concept. It can be argued that merely stabilising such emissions at 1990 levels in 2000 – a commitment made by a Conservative government as long ago as 1992 – required little or no effort on the part of the government.

The Labour government in 1997 accepted the notion of sustainability as promoted by their Conservative predecessors. The Labour party in 1997 made a supererogatory and 'challenging' manifesto pledge unilaterally to cut carbon dioxide emissions by 20 per cent by 2010. The prime minister said after the election: 'Environmental considerations must be integrated into all our decisions', but the only real move then made towards achieving this was the establishment of an environmental audit committee in the Commons. When the minister, John Battle, introducing the DTI annual report on Energy in September 1997, set out the main principles of the government's energy policy, they resembled Wakeham's in many ways. The government wanted to ensure diverse, secure and sustainable supplies of energy, to encourage a smooth move to competition in gas and electricity markets, to provide informed choices for consumers along with giving greater weight to social issues and putting a higher priority on environmental protection.

Whether or not all of these were really assumed to be compatible, within less than three months the government became embroiled in the death throes of the British coal industry. The measures taken to mitigate the situation had a significant effect on the environmental objectives, providing a vivid demonstration of the impact of political pressures on environmental problems. The environmental field is one where notions of coherent policy – or 'joined up government' – seem most frequently to break down, because the problems of externalities are so hard to resolve. This is due to institutional factors, and to the many conflicting objectives which governments are trying to reconcile and the political pressures to which all governments are subject.

The permanent Royal Commission on Environmental Pollution had been set up as long ago as 1967 under the premiership of Harold Wilson. But it was not until 1992 after much consultation and procrastination that the decision was reached to set up an Environment Agency. Environmental protection cuts across a great many sectors and government departments including agriculture, transport, industry and perhaps most obviously, energy.

As a result of the agreement reached at Kyoto in 1997 it was the government's aim to have a full climate change programme in place by the time that the protocol was ratified (possibly in the year 2001). Half the reduction in carbon dioxide emissions from 1990 to 2000 was projected to come from the switch from coal to gas in the electricity supply industry. The rest would derive from increased nuclear productivity, renewables, energy efficiency programmes, increased use of combined heat and power schemes (CHP), reducing methane in landfills and annual increases above inflation in road fuel duties (Hodges, 1998), but in most cases this was not supported by definite policy innovation.

Carbon dioxide emissions in the UK were on a downward trend at the end of the 1990s, due to a decline in heavy industry; domestic and power station emissions were also falling, though those from road transport were rising. An overall increase was expected before 2010 in line with economic growth. As the scope for further fuel switching from coal to gas in power stations was reduced, and existing nuclear power stations were decommissioned and replaced, carbon dioxide emissions would rise again. These emissions are much harder to abate than those from sulphur or indeed CFCs which were such a cause for anxiety in the 1980s, but which proved amenable not only to substitution but to international agreement. Carbon dioxide is much more difficult to deal with than these; there is no affordable quick technical fix for carbon (TIC, Session 1997–8, HC 471, para. 18).

At virtually the same time as the Kyoto meeting was taking place, coal problems surfaced once more. The moratorium on consents for new gas fired power stations was intended to provide a level playing field for coal and the White Paper on energy sources published in October 1998 was a response to this. Diversity was the main theme. It was but one of many reviews of energy and sustainability. At much the same time, the climate change consultation paper and Marshall report were a response to the need to meet the Kyoto obligations. How the Kyoto targets were to be met, whether the 20 per cent cut in carbon dioxide emissions really meant anything, how far measures needed to meet the climate change targets were compatible with competitive markets and what use should be made of energy taxes and the like were questions which remained unanswered (Parker, 1998). Security and diversity of energy supplies cannot easily be reconciled with competitive prices and sustainability. Equity also presents problems and the key challenge remained the domestic sector.

The structure of regulation after privatization reinforced the tendency to sideline environmental concerns. From being public service organizations, the privatized firms had become profit-making ones with economic regulators. As a result, the environmental issues were initially given a low priority and like the social agenda discussed in Chapter 3, only came into prominence later. Policies to control externalities will often increase production costs, so the logic of environmental regulation works in the opposite direction to that of price regulation. It is not difficult to see that problems are likely to arise when there are two regulators with responsibility for the same industry, since their duties are quite different. A regard for the environment was originally a secondary duty for all the economic regulators. The 1989 Electricity Act for instance had no direct reference to environmental issues, though the regulator had to take into account 'the environmental effects of generation, transmission and supply'. Similar wording applied to the other regulators. The water regulator has more specific environmental duties under the Environment Act 1995 covering conservation of flora and fauna, which also placed a duty on the companies to promote the efficient use of water by their customers, but where a conflict occurred, competition was to override other considerations. In addition he has to deal not only with the Environment Agency (EA) but also with the Drinking Water Inspectorate (DWI) which is part of the DETR. The lines of demarcation here are clearer than for the energy regulator. The energy efficiency standards of performance (EESoPs) and the obligation to work towards ten per cent of energy from renewables are also included in the new legislation. OFTEL does not have much to do in this area as relatively little environmental blight is caused by telecoms, though transmitter masts for mobile phones have spread across the landscape, usually with no need for planning permission.

Pollution control and environmental protection are based on the principles of BATNEEC (best available technology not entailing excessive cost) and BPEO (best practicable environmental option). The vagueness of these principles causes immense problems. In the environmental field, therefore, the same sorts of issues arise as in other aspects of utility regulation: the question of how much discretion the regulator has or should have; the difficulty of communication between different regulators and government departments, including the Treasury; and the problem of reconciling the demands of different agencies and the public. In the course of this chapter examples from each of gas, electricity and water will be used to illustrate these problems.

The EA was formed in 1995 from the amalgamation of the National Rivers Authority (NRA), Her Majesty's Inspectorate of Pollution (HMIP) and some local authority waste authorities. The NRA was much larger than the others and came to be the dominant force (Helm, 1998a, p. 15). The total workforce is around 9,000. Not surprisingly, the disparate arms of the EA have very different objectives.

The Environment Agency's chief purpose is to 'protect and enhance the environment' and to 'contribute to sustainable development'. The major part of its wide-ranging duties and powers involve managing the water environment, including flood control. Its remit also includes controlling pollution from industrial processes and regulating most power generating capacity but only some industrial users. There is no doubt though that the EA's heart is in water; air quality is more of an added extra. It has no responsibility for domestic energy use. Each of its predecessor bodies had its own history, structure and methods of working. HMIP, descended from the autonomous Alkali Inspectorate set up in the 1870s, focuses on emission control. The inspectors are chemists or chemical engineers and tend to operate in an informal way, often closely linked with particular firms or sectors. The total work force is only about 400.

The NRA on the other hand, is a recent creation, a result of the privatisation of the water companies and the hiving off of their regulatory activities. It could not have been more different from the pollution inspectorate, with a workforce of 8,000 consisting of biologists whose approach was far more legalistic. Furthermore, as the first chairman of the NRA, Lord Crickhowell, commented, it was not just a regulator but the manager of a major resource (Carter and Lowe, 1995, p. 44). It was also part of a wide-ranging network of interests, including not only the government departments already mentioned but other non departmental bodies such as English Nature, the NFU, the CLA, water companies and of course Ofwat (Carter and Lowe, 1995, p. 58). In spite of this, the agency was established with no separation between operations such as flood defence on the one hand and regulation and enforcement on the other. For the first time, however, there was a duty to take account of the costs and benefits of its activities; but the agency, which often appeared to be reluctant to judge its work by economic criteria (their staff included only five economists), devised its own technique in preference to cost benefit analysis.

Unlike the regulators of gas, electricity and water, the agency has not had a high profile director, and as a result has not had the same status or input into policy-making. Being viewed by some as merely a pollution control agency, there is a danger of its becoming a lobbyist of the Environment department rather than being at the centre of the process.

This somewhat haphazard institutional structure is mirrored in the DETR, formerly the DoE, which was established in 1970. Described by Peter Hennessy as 'the classic quangoid department' (Hennessy, 1990, p. 440), its remit includes housing, transport and water but not energy which is the responsibility of the Department of Trade and Industry. As a result, there is no government department that has overall charge of environmental policy. The environmental audit committee, set up in November 1997, showed up in its first few reports the lack of co-ordination in many aspects of government policy.

An important distinction in the discussion of environmental measures is that between methods designed to control the pollution of natural resources, for instance nitrates in water, and those intended to prevent or slow down their over exploitation such as over-abstraction. The control of pollution can be achieved in a variety of ways. The oldest and simplest – command and control – involves setting a level of permissible pollution, possibly issuing licences. This approach obviously needs inspection and enforcement and is more appropriate for hazardous and complex materials such as nuclear waste; and has the drawback of being vulnerable to 'technical capture' by experts (Helm, 1998a, p. 10).

Other methods are based on more positive incentives. These include taxation of various kinds and more market based approaches such as tradeable permits. Straightforward taxes raise the question: is an energy tax a means of raising revenue or of reducing pollution by cutting down on the use of fossil fuels? The answer is 'both' of course, but the former motive often seems to predominate; however, if the tax is successful in its environmental objective it will produce less revenue over time. In fact, the more successful it is the less revenue it will produce.

The key difference between command and control and economic instruments is one of information. The action or effect of economic instruments *reveals* information where command and control methods require the gathering of much data. Little has been done so far in the

UK in the way of introducing such means of pollution control; the landfill tax is one of very few examples. Carbon taxes would have the effect of providing incentives to consumers to use less fuel, to producers to switch fuels and even encourage greater research and development into carbon free fuels (Helm, 1998a). The difficulties are largely political.

The climate change levy

This policy innovation, a new departure for the UK, was announced in the November 1998 pre-budget report and provides an illuminating example of the pitfalls – many of them political in character – encountered in attempting to impose a tax on energy. In pursuit of the Kyoto targets, Lord Marshall formerly of BA, was asked to consider whether energy efficiency could be improved and greenhouse gases reduced by means of economic instruments such as an energy tax. He outlined the criteria that he considered essential, which included that the tax should broadly be based on the carbon content of fuel and that there should be some recycling of revenues to energy efficiency schemes. But his report also called for all sectors to contribute and a range of economic instruments to help bring this about, including a system of tradeable permits, which could provide valuable experience in testing new approaches and even provide greater efficiency.

The 1999 budget included the firm proposal that such a tax should be imposed from 2001; it was estimated that it could contribute up to 30 per cent of the Kyoto target. There was a huge negative reaction from business and industry. The exclusion of the domestic and road transport sectors was widely seen as unfair; the description of the tax as 'revenue neutral' was criticised, since the funds raised were to be used for a reduction in employers' national insurance contributions across the board. The high energy users do not in general employ large numbers, so they would not benefit from the reduction nearly as much as the labour intensive service industries, which would in effect be handed a subsidy. Rebates on the tax for higher energy users were provided for; agreements on energy efficiency improvements between companies or trade associations were to be negotiated; £50 million of the proceeds would fund energy efficiency projects and renewables. The levy would be based on the 'energy' use, not carbon content, thus mitigating the effect on coal and reducing the targeting on carbon so there would be no incentive to switch fuels. CHP schemes were not to be exempted. Nor were there any firm plans for tradeable permits.

The levy was described as 'Unfair, badly thought out and a serious threat to competitiveness' (*Financial Times*, 28 May 1999). The proposed rebates, some argued, simply exposed the contradictions in the policy: 'a triumph of political fudge over environmental need' (*Utility Week*, 16 April 1999). Suspicions were directed at the Treasury, where it was thought raising revenue had possibly been given a higher priority than environmental improvements. Months of ferocious lobbying resulted in significant concessions on many points to the motoring lobby and to heavy industry, which reduced the projected take from £1.75 to £1 billion. CHP and renewables were to be exempt after all. All revenues would be fully recyclable. Discounts of up to 80 per cent were available to those who reached energy efficiency agreements. As John Horam, chairman of the Environment Audit Committee commented, 'The Treasury is still almost an environment free zone' (*Financial Times*, 22 Feb. 1999). Thus not for the first time, the hard choices were postponed. A carbon tax, though more effective than an energy tax, would also have disadvantages since it would increase the incentives to switch from coal and oil to gas and nuclear power. Politically, to hit coal and encourage nuclear energy would be problematic and this could be the real reason for avoiding a carbon tax.[1]

Alternatives to taxation

There are also 'no regrets' policies, which would in retrospect still appear to have been worthwhile even if the impact of global warming was negligible. The most obvious of these are energy efficiency measures, such as insulation, which will save money even if they are not needed to save the world. Not that improved energy efficiency is always an energy saving policy; the contribution that can be made to energy saving by such schemes as the government-funded Home Energy Efficiency Scheme is uncertain since the fuel poor tend to take the benefit as increased comfort.

Economic instruments other than taxation tackle pollution in a different way. Tradeable permits for instance reduce the need for the large quantities of information, which are required for taxation and command and control methods. First promoted in the 1960s for dealing with air pollution, they are provided for in the Kyoto protocol, which plans for a global market in carbon dioxide.

Kyoto provides for three mechanisms by which this maybe done. Joint Implementation allows developed countries to 'buy' emissions reductions that have taken place in other developed countries as a way to meet part of their targets. The Clean Development Mechanism allows developed countries to sponsor a project abroad and gain a credit. Then there is emissions trading which allows those who have exceeded their targets to sell the excess (DTI, 1999, p. 40).

Although it led the way in introducing free market principles in energy markets and has exercised a global influence in the field, the UK was slow to adopt the same principles for environmental regulation. The government took the view that this alternative would take too long to establish and might clash with an international permits scheme to be launched in 2008 as part of the Kyoto agreements and might be difficult to police. There are many complexities involved with setting up tradeable permit schemes; should permits be handed out to existing polluters or auctioned which would bring in revenue for the state? Strong penalties are necessary as under the command and control style. The draft climate change programme published in March 2000 did include the development of carbon trading, which must somehow be grafted on to the climate change levy.

The new energy efficiency standards scheme, also part of the overall programme, could be integrated with the trading scheme. The omission of the domestic sector and only voluntary arrangements for transport emissions, reflecting the lobbying that took place, enormously reduces the effectiveness of the climate change strategy. The target of ten per cent of electricity from renewables by 2010 is highly ambitious. The UK is once again behind some other European nations such as Holland, Germany and the Scandinavian countries. Renewables have been included in the fossil fuel levy since 1990 and are now its sole beneficiary, but the new electricity trading arrangements will not favour them.

The problems of taxing domestic energy consumption

In spite of the fact that about a third of carbon dioxide emissions are attributable to domestic energy use, increasing tax on domestic fuel became politically near to impossible at the end of the 1990s. In the Conservative budget of March 1993, Chancellor Norman Lamont announced the intention to extend VAT to gas and electricity starting in April 1994 with an 8 per cent rate, to rise to 17.5 per cent the following year. This was confirmed in November 1993 along with the introduction of various measures to compensate pensioners and low-income families including a rise in the basic pension, which in total would use up about 40 per cent of the revenue raised. However the rise in the VAT rate was defeated in the Commons the following year, so it remained at 8 per cent. Once elected, Labour reduced the 8 to 5 per cent, the minimum permissible under EU law. The road fuel duty escalator was also politically very unpopular; begun by Lamont at 5 per cent per annum and raised to 6 per cent by Labour Chancellor Gordon Brown, it was eased off in November 1999. Apart from the political unpopularity that will engulf any government that raises taxes so steeply in this way, it is also clear that pricing measures alone will not suffice to reduce demand for energy. The price elasticity of demand for petrol is so low that in order to alter consumer behaviour significantly, with rising incomes, increasingly heavy taxes would be required.

Measures here do not always pull in the same direction. For instance, the success of the liberalization of the domestic energy markets has chiefly been measured by the extent of fall of prices for domestic energy bills. This is also largely true of the success of the regulators, by the Directors General themselves as well as the government and the public. But it should not be forgotten that a fall in domestic energy prices leads to a rise in demand; it has been calculated that a 10 per cent fall in prices leads to a 1–2 per cent rise in demand, which will in turn result in a rise in emissions. A rise in the costs of domestic fuel bears much more heavily on the low-income groups and thus resembles a regressive tax; for petrol similar measures are less regressive, though they would hit poorer people in rural areas.

Energy efficiency and the E-Factor

The UN Convention on Climate Change, signed at Rio in 1992, committed the United Kingdom, as earlier noted, to returning greenhouse gas emissions to 1990 levels by the year 2000. Priority was given to carbon dioxide. Action was to be voluntary. The Energy Saving Trust (EST) was established by the government to provide financial resources for the promotion of energy efficiency to meet the Rio targets. The trust was the central feature of this policy and was intended to contribute one quarter of the programme (Manners, 1995, p. 156).

The first gas regulator, Sir James McKinnon had in 1991 started a scheme to promote energy efficiency. Known as the E-Factor, this was used by British Gas to pass on to customers the costs of investment in energy efficiency measures, since the RPI−X formula did not incorporate an energy efficiency incentive. From the setting of the new price formula in 1992 it included a levy to raise finance for such projects. It was expected to raise £400 million for the EST by the end of the decade. Little controversy was aroused about this till the appointment of Clare Spottiswoode who succeeded McKinnon in November 1993.

In 1994 British Gas proposed five projects under the E-Factor scheme. Though the promotion of efficiency in the use of gas was one of her secondary duties, Ms Spottiswoode would not give permission for these. She had already made it clear to the Select Committee on the Environment, that in her opinion it was a levy on consumers, in effect a tax and that as an independent regulator, it was not for her to raise taxes. This was a matter for parliament, she maintained. The TIC generally agreed with this and the Trust took the view that the levy should be set by the Secretary of State who had an environmental duty under the gas and electricity legislation (TIC, Session 1994–5, HC 23, p. 53). The electricity regulator apparently did not have a problem with the parallel scheme for electricity and large sums of money were raised and spent on insulation and energy saving light bulbs through the Standards of Performance scheme. He did admit however, that he was aware of the fact that not all customers would benefit, and if the sum had been larger than the £100 m that was raised in this way it would be moving closer to fiscal policy (Prosser, 1997, p. 176).

In March 1994 Spottiswoode was cross-examined once more by the environment committee, and accused of 'driving a coach and horses through the government's energy saving strategy' by her refusal to continue with the sort of projects McKinnon had authorised (Environment Committee, 1994–5, HC 328, Q42). She told them that she believed in the targets for carbon dioxide emissions, but had no remit to further them, indeed no environmental remit at all – as an unelected person it was not up to her to do anything about it. She went so far as to say that her predecessor had exceeded his legal powers, something she was later obliged to withdraw. She was grilled on her position several times by the environment committee, and continued to insist that her main reason for refusing to authorise the levy was the constitutional point of 'no taxation without representation'. She claimed that she held this view so strongly because of her Treasury training. She perceived it as illegal, once referring back to the Bill of Rights, even though the EST had been an election pledge. Both McKinnon and Littlechild took a different view. The committee was annoyed by her slowness in responding and went into the circumstances of her appointment at some length. There was some irritation that a person had been appointed who was so much at odds with government policy (Tierney, 1996, p. 15). Though not a matter of major public controversy, Spottiswoode's insistence on sticking to what she perceived as her duty represented another moment when the extent of the discretion of the regulators was seriously called into question.

However, Ms Spottiswoode's point of view was quite widely shared. The revenue raising powers implied in the establishment of these schemes were politically and economically unrealistic (Chesshire, 1996, p. 357). The introduction of VAT on domestic fuel announced in November 1993 caused the GCC to reconsider its support for the E-Factor. Should customers be forced to contribute up to £400 m to the EST? The council took the view that if it was to continue the levy should appear as a separate item on customers' bills (GCC, 1993, p. 20). The TIC in its report on Energy Regulation made it a recommendation that the government should accept responsibility for raising any levies on gas consumers to fund energy efficiency measures (TIC, Session 1996–7, HC 50, para. 118).

By refusing to implement the E-factor scheme, Ms Spottiswoode not only put a stop to energy efficiency schemes, but also in addition helped to ensure that competition in the gas market was purely on price. As a result the expected energy service companies offering packages with advice on energy efficiency did not develop (TIC, Session 1997–8, HC 338, p. 134). Several years later, on the eve of the Kyoto conference, she was questioned once more. Still of the same opinion, she repeated that it was her job to get the best possible prices for consumers and for the government to decide whether to take up in taxes some or all of the reduction in prices. All she had at her command was a price control and now that the market was a competitive one she could not ask the incumbent to raise its prices.

> As soon as we start getting involved in other forms of regulation, whether it is income control, through directors' pay, or increasing taxes on energy for carbon emissions for example, we are really starting to usurp the role of parliament.
>
> (TIC, Session 1996–7, HC 50, Q 867)

By 1995 the DTI had admitted that the EST was no longer expected to contribute carbon savings on the scale originally envisaged. The electricity standards of performance, however, continued from 1994 to 1998 and at the end of 1999 the energy regulator, McCarthy, restarted the scheme. It was extended to gas and to second tier electricity suppliers at a rate of £1 per customer each year. The new Utilities legislation provided for the Secretary of State to set the levy at £1.20 per year for each customer, which it was calculated would raise £100 m in two years. It was estimated that the first scheme had lowered carbon dioxide emissions by six million tonnes and reduced electricity bills by £410 m (DTI, 1995, p. 59).

The two other cases considered here concern the impact of the actions of the environmental regulator: first on power companies and second on the water regulator. There is a good deal of game theory related literature on how two regulators interact (for example Baron, 1985). The EA as environmental regulator has to achieve a balance between cost on the one hand and pollution levels or environmental protection on the other. The electricity regulator has to price electricity based on the costs of production and of pollution control. The firm may have better information than either and may try to act strategically and play them off against each other. This kind of situation can apply for electricity or water. The theoretical work on this suggests that the environmental regulator will prefer non-cooperation as it results in higher expenditure on pollution control. Co-operative behaviour is likely to be favoured by the economic regulator since it would reduce such expenditure, thus keeping prices to consumers lower.

Electricity generators and the EA

The electricity regulator, OFFER, was supposed to promote efficiency and economy in the use of electricity and also take account of the environmental effects of generation and supply, but had no active role in environmental protection, and sought none. As a rule there was little communication between the economic regulators for gas and electricity and the EA, apart from occasionally on emissions from power stations. Just how limited contact was between these agencies is indicated by the fact that the EA did not send OFFER and Ofgas important documents such as the White Paper on Sustainable Development (TIC, Session 1996–7, HC 50, para. 112). The select committee enquiry into energy regulation in 1997 found that this lack of clarity had led to a situation in which no one body was prepared to take the lead; it was a case of 'passing the parcel' (HC 50, para. 108). There was pressure from environmental groups such as the RSPB and the WWF for a greater role for the DGs. The committee concluded that changes in powers for the economic regulators would only increase the confusion. What was needed was much improved co-operation and co-ordination and clarification of where responsibilities lay. By 1998 when a serious clash occurred, no such improvement had taken place.

Unlike carbon dioxide emissions, which did not become a salient practical issue until Rio, the acid rain problem had been on the European environmental agenda since the early 1980s (MacKerron and

Boira Segarra, 1996, p. 115). Sulphur dioxide is principally a by-product of burning coal to generate electricity and is the most important environmental issue for the generators and more than half of it comes from power stations. Before the electricity industry was privatised, dealing with sulphur limits was far simpler, since the CEGB was the only significant emitter. International negotiation became important and regulation took place at various levels, international, national and local. Her Majesty's Inspectorate of Pollution was established in 1987 to put in place Integrated Pollution Control (IPC) systems. This was based on the two concepts BATNEEC and BPEO. The first was rather imprecise, but much stricter on new investment than on existing plant and equipment. Long negotiations in the EC over the Large Combustion Plant Directive (LCPD) took place from the mid-1980s. The UK, sceptical about the damage caused by sulphur dioxide and nitrogen, had resisted joining the '30 per cent club' in 1985 but in 1988 agreed to reduce sulphur emissions gradually till 60 per cent were eliminated by 2003, and in 1994 agreed to further cuts (DTI, 1995, p. 56). Other EU members had more demanding targets than the UK on the understanding that it would achieve reduction mostly by means of fitting flue gas desulphurisation (FGD) equipment (TIC, Session 1992–3, HC 236, p. 254). Sulphur dioxide emitted from power stations can be eliminated by the FGD technique, but it requires quantities of limestone that must be quarried, thus posing another environmental dilemma, as well as using large amounts of water. Nor is it a particularly cheap way of cleaning up coal emissions, adding as much as one quarter to generation costs. But it was an available technique under the BATNEEC policy. The alternatives were to burn low sulphur imported coal or switch to gas.

In the event the dash for gas was to account for much of the reduction; targets were on course to be met without the installation of much FGD. The original plan to fit FGD to 12 GW of plant was reduced to only 6. Stricter limits were being brought in however, across all of Europe for the years 2005–10. The LCPD, though a European directive, was to be interpreted at national level by HMIP. Lengthy negotiations from 1993 to 1996 reached a measure of agreement on sulphur limits, both overall for each generator and site-specific for each plant. The companies were reluctant to fit FGD. While the inspectorate favoured it as the best available technique, the generators resisted this as excessively costly, especially as most of the power stations involved were old. In other words what was arrived at was a regime of more stringent limits rather than compulsory retrofitting of FGD. Given the reluctance of the generators to invest in FGD, the result would be running coal fired plant for less time (TIC, Session 1997–8, HC 404, para. 75). This represented another nail in coal's coffin with little discussion in parliament or in public. Drax, the monster power station owned by National Power and Ratcliffe, which belongs to PowerGen – representing 25 per cent of coal and oil fired capacity – were the only power stations with the equipment (6 GW in total). Although the CCGT plants displaced coal plant, at the same time their introduction postponed the binding of the constraint on burning coal in power stations without FGD, reducing the incentive to install it. The high capital cost involved meant that it was really only suitable for baseload plant with a life of at least ten years.

In March 1998, the Environment Agency, into which the HMIP was now incorporated, proposed a tightening of the 1996 plans for stricter limits on sulphur emissions (which had up till then been surpassed). It had been agreed that these should be cut by 84 per cent of the 1991 figure by 2005, which had produced some consternation; instead of 2005, it was now suggested that this target should be met by 2001. And so at a time when the government was exploring the issue of a 'level playing field' for coal, threats to the beleaguered coal industry appeared to be multiplying. The generators reacted angrily. PowerGen argued that the Environment Agency had not assessed the impact on the coal industry or on energy policy, and that the authorisations of 1996 should not be reviewed so soon, especially since a review of energy policy was under way. No costing had been done and BATNEEC had been improperly applied. It would mean the end of the coal industry. The Environment Agency's case was that the dash for gas and the longer life expectancy of the Magnox nuclear stations meant a larger than expected reduction in the demand for coal and therefore lower sulphur dioxide levels. The head of the agency defended the decision as a BATNEEC one. The agency wanted the FGD plants to run at full load all the time.

But the DTI still in some senses acted as a sponsor for the electricity industry as it had done in the days of nationalisation. The relationship remains a close one, because the regulator OFFER (now Ofgem) reports to the department, and for several years after the sell-off retained shares in the generators. The pollution inspectorate is at an informational disadvantage *vis-à-vis* the DTI and the generators and has little input into policy-making. It is worth noting that the privatisation prospectuses for National Power and PowerGen had included the information that at least eight gigawatts of capacity would have to be retrofitted with FGD. The reluctance of the two large generators to invest huge sums in FGD equipment can be attributed to the inevitable loss of market share which they faced, and the consequent need to diversify (Skea, 1995, p. 192).

This episode reveals a lack of communication and transparency between the generators and the EA; 'A dialogue of the deaf' said one MP (TIC, Session 1997–8, HC 404, p. 175). Not only that, but consultation with the government departments concerned had been quite inadequate. There had been little attempt to integrate energy and environmental priorities – 'rather than one being a tardy intrusion into the other' (TIC, Session 1997–8, HC 471-I, para. 21) in other words, not much joined up government. Also open to criticism were the generators, in particular PowerGen who had eventually fitted FGD at Ratcliffe but had not done so at Ferrybridge and Fiddler's Ferry in spite of having had £200 million of government money for the purpose at privatisation. These two plants, bought by Mission Energy were to be fitted with FGD with £120 million from PowerGen.

The conclusions of the power sources review announced in June 1998, following the TIC, favoured greater flexibility in the application of the rules on sulphur emissions. What remained was the commitment to the 2005 targets: a reversal of policy by the EA (DTI, 1998b, p. 78). The review recommended the addition of FGD equipment to one plant for each large generator, which should be used more intensively than the ordinary plant. The EA also introduced incentives to fit FGD. Eastern planned to fit cleaners at West Burton and Mission at the former PowerGen plants, but the net result was a slower move to cutting SO_2.

The fact that the dash for gas made the targets relatively easy to meet may have had the negative effect of relaxing efforts, on the part both of the government and its agencies and the various companies involved, towards energy saving and new research and development towards the abatement of carbon dioxide; and possibly even to the detriment of meeting those targets. Trying to make up lost ground in the early years of the new century will undoubtedly cost more and prove harder.

The 1999 water price review

In the case of water, the environmental pressures were rather different. The economic regulator, after years of rising prices, was keen to keep them stable while the environment regulator had an agenda of constant improvement. The relations between the Environment Agency and

Ofwat were combative and the fact that the two regulators were in separate agencies meant that the debate was forced out into the open (Prosser, 1997, p. 298). From the start, there was a conflict between the need to spend huge sums on infrastructure to renew outworn systems and to bring them up to European standards and the regulator's insistence on willingness to pay and affordability. The trade off between these two is sustainability in practice. To complicate matters, introducing environmental regulation means introducing EU influence. European directives such as those on Bathing Beaches and Urban Waste Water are responsible for the huge sums which have had to be spent by English water companies. This meant that instead of an RPI−X price control, as for the other utilities there was RPI+K and prices rose hugely over the first few years. Byatt publicly criticised those standards. His firmly held line throughout the 1994 review was that of willingness to pay (Prosser, 1997, p. 121). Some of the expenditure to improve quality was unnecessary in his view and the pressure for it originated in the EU, even though the subsidiarity principle should permit the UK to choose a lower level of expenditure. The previous review had seen some skilful manoeuvring by the water companies and the result had been that they had spent well below the projected amounts and still improved their performance.

In the 1999 review, a reasonable level of co-operation was achieved (Helm, 1998b), though it often seemed like a trial of strength, or a 'game of poker' in the words of one Ofwat economist. In October 1996, Byatt, determined that at last the customer should see an end to rising prices, at least temporarily, pre-empted any plans that the EA might have had when he announced the pattern at the start of the process: a one off cut in prices, known as a P-nought adjustment. This was supported by the ONCC. He made no indication of what annual price change he sought. The EA, whose first opportunity it was to influence the process, took a different view. It wanted a result which took 'full account of future environmental needs and should not be set at a predetermined limit' (Streeter, 1999, p. 185). The agency favoured an annual price increase level with the retail price index – that is a zero figure for X – and also made it clear that it was an independent regulator that was part of the review process and would advise ministers.

The procedure was that the Secretary of State received advice on those improvements thought advisable by the agency and the Drinking Water Inspectorate, and also considered the open letter from the DG of Ofwat. One problem was that programme of works that the EA had decided should be carried out had costs attached but not benefits. The agency eschewed conventional cost benefit analysis in favour of a tool of its own devising, multi-attribute technique, or MAT (Helm, 1998b). Nor did it attach priorities to the various projects or provide any information on the implications for household bills.

The two year long process leading up to the 1999 review included meetings of a 'Quadripartite' group which included the DETR, Ofwat, the EA, and water companies, which was not a decision-making body but one which had been set up to ensure proper information was shared. One feature of the review was the battle for public opinion. Several parties commissioned a wide variety of market research. Survey results seemed to give the lie to Byatt's claim that what people most wanted was reduced bills. They also saw environmental improvements as important, though many took the view that the cost should be spread over future years. Byatt supported the view that future investment programmes should reflect the views of the public and the advice of the secretaries of state, while the EA preferred to give greater weight to the opinions of experts. But his final prices did not fully fund the EA's programme. Ultimately the government stepped in, added £1 billion to capital expenditure and reduced the size of the price cuts slightly, and since an election would be due by 2002, ruled out price rises at about that time. This is what Helm has described as the environmental tax 'wedge' (Helm, 1998a, p. 13). It is implicit environmental taxation that falls on the customer.

The clash between environmental and social policy can be adjusted by means of the benefits system; Norman Lamont tried to do this in 1993–4 when he introduced taxes on domestic electricity and gas. But the self-imposed restraints which governments now work under in relation to the PSBR and the determination not to increase income tax severely limit what can be done (Helm, 1998a, p. 12). The energy efficiency levy strongly opposed by Clare Spottiswoode (and indeed the nuclear levy that lasted from electricity privatisation until 1998) were in effect hypothecated taxes which pre-dated Gordon Brown's windfall tax in 1997.

The environmental field shows up emphatically the problems of policy co-ordination and how fatally easy it is for governments to compromise long-term goals. But the real difficulty is that 'Without an organising concept and a clear objective, environmental policy in practice collapses into a series of ad hoc measures, driven as much by the relative political weight of other considerations, as by environmental concerns' (Helm 1998a, p. 17).

7
'Governments in Miniature'?

'There are no solutions to problems, only a process of policy succession which requires the capacity to learn from mistakes.'*

The preceding chapters have described in turn the various aspects of an interlocking system that, though it is often or usually dealing with economic issues, is essentially political. The regulators have to balance the demands of competing interests. 'Political decision making is rendered difficult because of its having to deal with conflicting legitimate claims' (Wolin, 1961, p. 272). As Chapter 1 showed, the network utility industries nationalized in the late 1940s eventually became, as a result of multiple objectives and inadequate accountability, subject to excessive political influence. As a reaction to this, the privatization of the utilities by the Conservative governments of the 1980s and 1990s was based on the concept of regulation by independent but accountable regulators. Their main focus was intended to be economic.

The passing of a new Utilities Act in 2000, even a partly dismembered one, marks the end of a first phase which has been characterized by steep learning curves and considerable achievements as well as some setbacks and failures. These achievements include the acquisition of a great deal of expertise by the regulators. Clare Spottiswoode saw her role as resembling that of the chairman of a company; regulation, she said, was an entrepreneurial activity (PAC, Session 1996–7, HC 89, para. 82). It would not be an overstatement to say that a process of discovery has been taking place since BT was privatized in 1984; much has been learnt by regulators, companies and consumers.

*The title of the chapter is taken from Prosser, 1997, p. 305; the epigraph is from Rhodes, 1994, p. 151.

In the beginning the chief rationale was economic efficiency and this has been enormously improved, but a price was paid in many lost jobs. For instance, British Gas shed more than 40 per cent of its workforce between 1990 and 1995 (TIC, Session 1996–7, HC 50, para. 38). The electricity industry lost 32,000 jobs between 1989 and 1994 (Lascelles, 1995, p. 31). There had been considerable over-manning, but some of those who lost their jobs would have been re-employed as the companies introduced outsourcing. The coal industry too was reduced to a fraction of its former size, the consequence not only of environmental regulation, but also of the structure of the privatized electricity industry; and the government at the very least showed a lack of concern at the effect on coal. Overall, studies suggest that gains and losses are fairly evenly balanced (Green and McDaniel, 1998). Prices of electricity and gas have fallen and the quality of service has risen in most cases. An analysis of the restructuring and privatization of the CEGB found that a permanent cost reduction had been achieved, but the gains had gone to the producers rather than consumers or the government (Newbery and Green, 1997, p. 299).

Many outside observers, as well as those more closely involved in utility regulation in the UK, took the view that this should be an economic exercise pure and simple. This is the gospel as preached by Littlechild, and accepted by some economists from both ends of the political spectrum. For instance, Christopher Foster, the 'arch privatizer' who was mentioned in Chapter 2, was of the opinion that a regulator is more likely to retain his independence if he narrows his task to economic regulation (Foster, 1992, p. 368). Social aspects should be left to ministers. This position was close to that of Carsberg in the early years at OFTEL. In spite of fairly onerous social obligations, he always favoured competition and could not approve of a pricing policy that might be seen as redistributing income. Certainly he wanted to go no further than the provisions of the 1984 Telecommunications Act. He could not properly propose a rule that all people on low incomes should be given telephones free of rental – that would involve 'arbitrary judgements about matters of income distribution' (Prosser, 1997, p. 64) – and such judgements should presumably be left to the politicians.

Some time later and from a rather different political viewpoint, Lord Currie seemed to share this opinion. It would be unfortunate, he said, if a Labour government impeded the introduction of competition or required the regulators to take distributional considerations into account. These are better dealt with through the tax and benefit system and 'it is best if regulators have focused objectives, to avoid problems of regulatory capture, unaccountability and uncertainty' (Currie, 1997, p. 7).

Though in its earliest form for BT and British Gas, a privatized utility meant a monopoly or near monopoly, competition was an integral component of the Littlechild doctrine. Price regulation, the argument ran, was a stopgap, intermediate instrument. Competition would eventually replace RPI − X; and, urged on by the regulators, this has happened. Competition, albeit in a non-Schumpeterian form, is present in gas, electricity and telecoms. Incumbents still have the lion's share of the market in all three industries but though many consumers have remained with their original supplier, there is now a choice. Competition in water, so long a distant prospect, is now beginning in the large market over 50 megalitres and it is believed will 'trickle down' to smaller users. Price caps began to wither away when Ofgem ended the price cap for both electricity and gas prices for direct debit users in April 2000 and was planning to do so for other customers in 2001. Oftel, on the other hand, having earlier suggested that the 1997 cap might be the last one, decided on a continuation after 2001. The introduction of competition, however, meant more not less regulation; detailed supervision of marketing and pricing strategies and efforts to level the playing field for the less well off and vulnerable consumers. Price regulation is likely to be transferred more and more to the essentially monopolistic networks of pipes and wires.

So regulation for social reasons is growing. As Foster himself presciently noted 'even if one political generation puts economic efficiency first, the passing of time and new exigencies of state make it likely that there will eventually be political interference that will subvert the primacy of that end' (Foster, 1992, p. 408).

This is of course what happened as the Labour opposition prepared itself for government in the mid-1990s. Initially utterly opposed to privatization, and indeed committed to renationalization without compensation, though its presentation was weak, the party gradually modified its position over the years. Eventually it came, as the Conservative party had in the 1950s, to accept the seismic shift in policy that had taken place. The 1992 manifesto was much vaguer on the utilities than in 1987, apart from a commitment to renationalize the NGC and the water industry. By the general election of 1997, partly as a result of the abandonment of Clause 4 of the constitution, the party had developed an approach that reconciled it with the privatization of the utilities, including the RPI − X form of price regulation. This was done in two ways. First there was the idea of the windfall tax, originally conceived by John Smith in 1993 and elaborated later by Gordon Brown during 1995 when public opinion had been much taken up with the controversy over the salaries paid to the directors of privatized companies. This, as remarked earlier, had the double benefit of penalizing the companies and benefiting the young unemployed. The windfall tax was one of five promises printed on a card and handed to party members, which included the words 'keep this card and see that we keep our promises' (Currie, 1997, p. 13). Secondly, there was the commitment to put the consumer at the heart of regulation. Thus social policy was the lynch pin of the new Labour approach to the utilities.

But notwithstanding the views of those who prefer a more purely economic form of regulation, social obligations had in fact always played a large part in the legislation. The regulators' primary duties included looking after consumers who might suffer from some disadvantage. The requirement to supply public telephones, for example or to have regard to the need of the pensioner or the disabled, pre-dates privatization. Universal service obligations in electricity, and restrictions on disconnection go back as far as 1899 (Prosser, 1997, p. 149). Nor is regulation about to wither away. On the contrary, a detailed panoply of regulations is being constructed. The regulator will have more to do. The social concerns to which the Labour government has devoted so much attention are reinforced by EU law (Prosser, 1997, p. 305). This is even truer of environmental regulation.

The conflict between the introduction of competition in the domestic market and the stronger emphasis on the consumer, especially the disadvantaged consumer, was not seriously addressed by the Labour Party until after the 1997 election, though as Chapter 3 related this became a matter of some public debate. But as we saw in Chapter 5, far from stopping the progress to liberalization of the domestic electricity market, the party pushed ahead with it in spite of the huge costs and the fact that the possible savings for consumers were more limited than in gas. This approach was foreshadowed in an IPPR book, Energy '98, which concluded that there was no point in looking back to a monopolistic world, 'we probably could not get the genii back in the bottle' (Corry et al., 1996, p. 122).

Regulation, whether of monopoly or for competition, was intended to be carried out by independent appointees, at 'arm's length'. After the extremes of political intervention that had been reached in the early 1980s, it was considered important to distance the new offices from government. The independence of the regulators and the large discretion given to them was a frequent focus of criticism in the past.

But that was the point; they were intended to be independent of government. The original legislation gave the regulators wide powers notwithstanding extensive ministerial rights to intervene or indeed to direct them, which were never used. They were to exercise their powers in the manner they considered best calculated to fulfil their duties; and were not obliged in many cases to give reasons, something which was frequently criticised by the Trade and Industry select committee but defended by the department under the Conservatives.

However, though they are non-ministerial departments, the regulators are clearly part of government; their website addresses are evidence of that. Their offices are largely staffed by civil servants. But to a great extent the individuals concerned succeeded in retaining their independence, and sometimes publicly disagreed with government policy. Though the government sought their advice on its implementation, their disapproval of the windfall tax was well known. Clare Spottiswoode deliberately flouted government policy on energy efficiency. Littlechild and McCarthy both made it clear that they disapproved of the restricted consents policy for gas fired power plants. Spottiswoode and Littlechild, like the various OFTEL regulators, adhered strongly to the point of view that competition was the correct way to bring prices down and benefit consumers. The department also sought, but did not necessarily take, their advice on issues such as takeovers and mergers as Chapter 4 showed. They also made policy on their own account; the most obvious instance was the licence amendments on which both the water and electricity regulators insisted in the case of multi-utility mergers. These amendments were framed so as to ensure ring fencing of accounts and safeguard regulation (Prosser, 1997, p. 137). Regulating access to pipes and wires has also been an important part of their work. Valuable expertise was gained on the workings of their industries; on technical issues, and accounting for comparative competition, for instance, with which the general competition authorities would not be able to compete. A more notorious example was Littlechild's attitude at the time of the coal crisis in 1992–3, when he refused to take any general responsibility for energy policy. The Northern Ireland regulator also took a very independent line when he ignored the recommendations of the MMC.

McCarthy's directorship at Ofgem is different from those of his two predecessors. In taking on board the social action plan he has faced up to a major challenge. The original document produced by Spottiswoode and Littlechild was thin and unenthusiastic. His onslaught on the electricity generators when he introduced a 'good behaviour' clause to control electricity spikes shows how regulation has changed since

Littlechild imposed a two-year price cap in 1994. Today there is a greater emphasis on process rather than outcome, which gives the regulator more leverage and ties in with the strengthening of competition law. After an initial decision by most of the companies to refer the matter to the Competition Commission, all but two decided to accept the new clause.

Though not party appointments, the regulators have generally been in sympathy with the government which appointed them – apart perhaps from Spottiswoode on the question of energy efficiency levies – and the series of new appointments which took place after the 1997 election was quite noticeable. Ian Byatt the water regulator, whose contract had already been renewed once, remained until the end of his contract in mid-2000, but the others, including Spottiswoode, Littlechild and the rail regulator John Swift, did not have their contracts renewed.

The Department of Trade and Industry has often appeared not to have a coherent policy on utility matters. This may partly be due to the fast turnover in secretaries of state – there have been 14 in 20 years. There are still 7 ministers at the DTI even though all the nationalised industries are now in the private sector. Not surprisingly ministerial intervention is quite frequent and sometimes seems to be prompted by short-term political motives. One example of this is the request in March 1999 from Stephen Byers to Callum McCarthy on standing charges. These accounted, he said, for around 13 per cent of a typical bill and could be as much as 20 per cent for those who used relatively little electricity. There was also a wide variation around the country and depending on method of payment. This was part of his newly launched 'knowledgeable consumers' campaign. 'This government', he said, was 'putting consumers at the heart of our policy agenda' and he wanted to ensure that the poor and pensioners were not at a disadvantage (DTI press release, 10 March 1999). This was a matter on which he had no formal powers and indeed the gas and electricity regulator was developing the social action plan. BGT subsequently abolished standing charges, but the new tariff, while benefiting low users, will disadvantage a large majority of the fuel poor.

DTI intervention in mergers policy has also been open to criticism. Two successive Secretaries of State have proposed removing decisions on mergers from the political sphere, which would be comparable with the Chancellor Gordon Brown's decision immediately on taking office in 1997 to hand over decisions on interest rates to the monetary policy committee of the Bank of England. The complex series of interactions involving the DTI, the regulator, the DGFT, the mergers panel, the

Competition Commission and the Secretary of State could become simpler and less open to lobbying.

The reforms introduced in 2000 after extensive consultation, and following the 1998 Green Paper, were aimed at countering these criticisms and giving as already mentioned a more prominent part to consumers. The sections of the Bill relating to water and telecoms were withdrawn at a late stage, but a new Bill for each industry was promised. Some of the provisions of the new legislation had been called for by academics, parliamentarians and practitioners for several years. The individual regulator will be replaced by a three-person regulatory authority, the gas and electricity markets authority, GEMA, to avoid the very personalised style that developed under the first generation of regulators. It will be obliged to give reasons for its decisions and will also have a requirement to have regard to the interests of low-income consumers. But there have also been some changes that extended regulatory discretion, and added the possibility of greater ministerial intervention, without augmenting accountability. The new principal objective, downgrading the financing requirement, is to protect the interests of consumers, wherever appropriate by promoting effective competition. And far from curbing regulatory discretion, the new provisions appeared to extend it. Along with new duties, there are new powers to adapt the licensing regime and impose heavy penalties on companies. The only restriction on regulatory power introduced is the requirement not to disregard the recommendations of the Competition Commission.

The commitment of the government to social regulation was underlined by the unexpected addition of a reserve power for the Secretary of State to raise a subsidy for disadvantaged consumers for energy bills if other measures prove inadequate, and the regulator's duty to have regard to the social and environmental objectives of the government. Measures which have significant financial implications will have to be referred to Parliament.

The proclaimed intention of the new legislation was to provide more predictable, transparent and accountable regulation but no order of preference is prescribed for this wide array of responsibilities. Government 'guidance', it appears, is rather vague and is certainly not 'direction', but includes taking account of government policy on improving the health of the nation and reducing the number of sub-standard houses. Such bland generalities provide scope for great discretion on the part of the regulator.

Environmental guidance in particular is so vague as to amount once again to mere lip service, in spite of the large gestures on reducing carbon dioxide emissions made by the government. 'Economic regulation of the utility industries does not take place in a vacuum…this means that economic regulation should be conducted in a way which is alert to the Government's wider social and environmental goals and where possible supportive of them.' The regulator has to have regard to the need for energy efficiency and the government's target of 10 per cent of energy being supplied by renewables by 2010. The Kyoto targets also form part of the guidance, but there is no mention of consultation between the environmental regulators and Ofgem, which remains inadequate.

Their workload is likely to increase and the controversies will not go away. On the social agenda, redistribution is by no means acceptable to all. Pressure groups such as the Public Utilities Access Forum want more than is likely to be conceded – such as weekly payments for utility bills at no extra charge. Precise targeting is a difficult task. Many will not welcome large expenditure on environmental measures, which may well be charged to utility customers rather than taxpayers for political reasons (Helm, 1999).

Accountability then remains less than satisfactory. There is political intervention for short-term reasons. The objectives of the regulators are many and broadly defined. The government hands down 'guidance'. Has the wheel come full circle? Has the new institution of a regulatory office reverted in less than 20 years to the style that prompted the privatization programme? This would probably be too pessimistic. The regulated companies are at one remove from government and they have shareholders. The primary duty is to consumers, who demand accountability as much from the company as from the regulator. The introduction of a board to replace the single regulator may safeguard independence as well as preventing a strongly personalized style. Above all, transparency has improved beyond all recognition and the new Act requires collective consideration among the regulators on matters of common interest and publication of the results. This might turn out to be a genuine improvement and should ensure consistency. At the time of writing, it remains to be seen how the regulators will use their new powers to be granted under the Utilities Act and the forthcoming legislation for water and telecommunications. But if it is to be a success, regulation must be more than 'a political fight between regulators, consumers, regulated companies and shareholders' (Prosser, 1997, p. 4). Success or failure will depend on the regulators as much as the government.

Notes

1 From Nationalization to Privatization

Regulatory capture: The capture of the regulator by the industry he regulates has taken place when he or she has adopted the goals and interests of the company as his own; when he is 'the prisoner of the facts as presented by the industry' (Foster, 1992, p. 204).

2 Regulators at Work

1. *Regulators and the dates they held office*:
   Sir Bryan Carsberg, Oftel, 1984 to March 1993.
   Don Cruickshank, Oftel, April 1993 to March 1998.
   David Edmonds, Oftel, from April 1998.
   Sir James McKinnon, Ofgas, 1986 to October 1993.
   Clare Spottiswoode, Ofgas, November 1993 to October 1998.
   Stephen Littlechild, Offer, September 1989 to December 1998.
   Callum McCarthy, Ofgem, from November 1998.
   Ian Byatt, Ofwat, August 1990 to July 2000.
   Philip Fletcher, Ofwat, from August 2000.
   Spottiswoode, Swift and Littlechild did not have their contracts renewed.
   Bridgeman was another casualty, his contract was not renewed in 2000.
   His successor is John Vickers, formerly a member of the Bank of England's
      Monetary Policy Committee.
2. *Austrian*: a school of economic thought founded in Vienna in the late nineteenth century. It emphasized competition as a process of discovery rather than a state of equilibrium. Those who hold these views tend to oppose regulation. See Burton, 1997.
3. *The electricity pool* was set up to provide a spot trading mechanism. All electricity was deemed to pass through the pool, even though much was covered by contracts. The prices at which electricity was bought and sold through the pool were determined for each half-hour on the basis of bids submitted by the generators. A secondary market existed in Contracts for Differences (CfDs). The pool was described as 'a theorists' creation' (Helm, in Energy Committee, Session 1991–2, HC 113, p. 56). Its workings were so complex that Industry Minister John Battle, giving evidence to the committee aptly, though perhaps not very originally, compared it with the Schleswig Holstein question. Only three people had ever understood it and one was dead, one had gone mad and the third had forgotten all he knew (TIC, Session 1997–98, HC 404, p. 67).
   The lack of transparency and high costs of administration plus the manipulative power that National Power and PowerGen were able to exercise as a result of their possession of most of the marginal plant led ultimately to the

decision of the Labour government to reform the system and introduce the new electricity trading arrangements, NETA.

4. *Present at the Creation*: This comes from Alphonso the Wise of Spain (1252–84), who is said to have remarked 'Had I been present at the Creation, I would have given some useful hints for the better ordering of the universe'.

5. *The Fossil Fuel Levy* was provided for in the Electricity Act 1989. Described as a 'rigid and opaque consumer tax' (MacKerron and Pearson, 1995, p. 251), the Levy was added to electricity prices to cover the difference between nuclear and renewable electricity and conventional generating costs. This chiefly meant nuclear capacity but also included some power from renewable sources, added to lend respectability to the levy. It continued till 1998 to compensate the RECs for their commitment – the NFFO or Non Fossil Fuel Obligation (NFFO) – to contract for some non-fossil fuel capacity. The levy was set at 11 per cent in 1992, reducing gradually after 1996.

6. *NETA*: the new electricity trading arrangements replace the electricity pool and its associated contracts market. It resembles other commodity markets, including the one for gas. Its features include direct contracting between customers and generators, thus permitting demand side bidding. There is also a screen based short term power exchange and a balancing mechanism. These new procedures are intended to address the previous bias against flexible generation plant, but doubts have been expressed about the likelihood of it combating the market power of the mid-merit generators. Integrated generators/suppliers will be best placed to manage the risks and this is likely to result in further integration in the ESI.

7. *Golden Shares*: held by the government, these were designed to prevent hostile takeovers by foreign companies and included powers over share issues, voting rights and disposal of assets. In the case of water companies and RECs, they expired in 1995. Most of the rest have now lapsed.

8. *The RECs' monopoly franchise*: At privatization in 1990 the RECs were given a monopoly franchise for all smaller customers in their area. These charges were price capped. The contract market for large customers (over 1 MW) was open to competition from the start. In 1994 this competitive market was extended to include those whose peak demand exceeded 100 kW. The franchise was abolished entirely in 1998–9 when the RECs lost their monopolies and the domestic market was also opened to competition.

3   A Fair Deal for Consumers?

1. Ninety-five per cent of households could have meters installed for an average cost of £200 but the remaining 5 per cent could cost up to £1,000 each. The variation in installation charges from one company to another is very wide.

4   Competition and Monopoly

1. *MMC Enquiries in the utility sector*:
   The dates given below relate to when the report was issued.

   Gas October 1988: possible existence of a monopoly situation.
   Telecoms February 1989: chatlines.

Water April 1990: Merger of General Utilities and Colne Valley Water Company and Rickmansworth Water Company.

Water July 1990: Southern Water plc and Mid Sussex Water Company merger.

Water July 1990: General Utilities plc and the Mid Kent Water Company merger.

Gas August and September 1993: Reports on double reference re supply of gas under Fair Trading Act and conveyance and storage of gas and fixing of tariffs under Gas Act 1986.

Electricity June 1995: Scottish Hydro-Electric; reference on price control.

Water July 1995: Lyonnaise des Eaux and Northumbrian Water plc merger.

Water July 1995: Portsmouth Water plc reference on charges.

Water July 1995: South West Water reference on charges.

Telecoms December 1995: Number Portability.

Electricity April 1996: National Power and Southern Electric plc, proposed merger.

Electricity April 1996: PowerGen plc and Midlands Electricity, proposed merger.

Water October 1996: Severn Trent and South West Water, proposed merger.

Water October 1996: Wessex Water and South West Water, proposed merger.

Electricity April 1997: Northern Ireland Electricity, reference on price control.

Gas June 1997: BG plc, prices for gas transportation and storage.

Electricity December 1997: Pacificorp and the Energy Group, proposed acquisition.

Telecoms January 1999: BT charges for calls to mobile phones.

2. *Tariff and contract customers*: The tariff or monopoly market was the section of the market for domestic and small users. These customers were charged according to prices – which might include a standing charge as well as a running rate – governed by the $RPI-X$ formula. Larger, contract customers negotiated with the supplier what their charges should be. Initially, the monopoly market was for supplies below 25,000 therms per year; this was reduced to 2,500 in 1992 and gradually abolished as domestic competition was introduced from 1996.

3. *RECs taken over 1995–9*:
July 1995 SWEB taken over by Southern Co., a US utility.
July 1995 Manweb taken over by Scottish Power.
July 1995 Eastern taken over by Hanson.
September 1995 Norweb taken over by North West Water.
November 1995 Seeboard taken over by Central and South West, a US utility.
November 1995 Swalec taken over by Welsh Water.
May 1996 Midlands taken over by Avon Energy, a US utility.
November 1996 Northern taken over by Calenergy, a US utility.
January 1997 Yorkshire taken over by American Power, a US utility.
September 1998 ScottishHydro merger with Southern Electric.
January 1999 London Electricity taken over by EdF.

Resales:
May 1998 Eastern, now Energy Group to TXU, a US utility.
July 1998 East Midlands to PowerGen.

May 1999 Swalec to British Energy.
June 1999 SWEB to London/EdF.
August 2000 Swalec to Scottish and Southern
Norweb to TXU.

4. *There is a lack of clarity about when or whether the government may overrule a* decision of the Commission. Cosmo Graham's opinion is that this has happened without argument when the reference was made under the Fair Trading legislation. See Graham, 1997, p. 224.

6   The Regulators and Parliament

1. *The economic purchasing obligation of the RECs*: meant that they could not buy more expensive electricity from a gas-fired station in which they had an interest. It was arguable that this did not mean that they had to buy the cheapest electricity available, but at the best price reasonably attainable given considerations of security, diversity etc. (Newbery and Green, 1996, p. 67).

7   'Governments in Miniature'?

1. *Carbon tax*: Sweden's 1991 carbon tax was severely modified after protests from energy intensive industries. The European community in 1992 also considered such a tax, but later modifications which purported to conserve energy as well as reduce carbon dioxide emissions in fact diluted the advantage to nuclear power and to those countries which relied heavily on it (Barrett, 1998, p. 25). There is a similar scheme in Denmark.

References

Abromeit, H. 1988, 'British Privatisation Policy', *Parliamentary Affairs*, Vol. 41, No. 1.

Armstrong, M., Cowan, S. and Vickers, J. 1994, *Regulatory Reform*, MIT, Cambridge, USA.

Ash, I. 1993, 'Obligations to Customers, Shareholders and the Community – a Company Perspective' in Hicks, *Utilities and their Customers: Whose Quality of Service is it?*

Baldwin, R. and McCrudden, C. (eds) 1987, *Regulation and Public Law*, Weidenfeld and Nicolson.

Barberis, P. 1998, 'The New Public Management and a New Accountability', *Public Administration*, Vol. 76, Autumn.

Baron, D. 1985, 'Noncooperative Regulation of a Nonlocalized Externality', *Rand Journal of Economics*, Vol. 16, No. 4, Winter.

Barrett S. 1998, 'Political Economy of the Kyoto Protocol', *Oxford Review of Economic Policy*, Vol. 14, No. 4.

Beckerman, W. 1991, 'Global Warming: a Sceptical Economic Assessment' in Helm, *Economic Policy Towards the Environment*.

Beesley, M. (ed.) 1992, *Privatisation, Regulation and Deregulation*, Routledge.

Beesley, M. (ed.) 1993, *Major Issues in Regulation*, IEA.

Beesley, M. (ed.) 1994, *Regulating Utilities: The Way Forward*, IEA.

Beesley, M. (ed.) 1995, *Utility Regulation: Challenge and Response*, IEA.

Beesley, M. (ed.) 1996, *Regulating Utilities: A Time for Change?* IEA.

Beesley, M. (ed.) 1997, *Regulating Utilities: Broadening the Debate*, IEA.

Beesley, M. (ed.) 1998, *Regulating Utilities: Understanding the Issues*, IEA.

Beesley, M. 1994, 'Abuse of Monopoly Power' in Beesley, *Regulating Utilities: the Way Forward*.

Beesley, M. and Laidlaw, B. 1995, 'The Development of Telecommunications Policy in the UK, 1981–1991', in Bishop et al., *The Regulatory Challenge*.

Beesley, M. and Littlechild, S. 1983, 'Privatisation: Principles, Problems and Priorities', *Lloyds Bank Review*, July.

Beesley, M. and Littlechild, S. 1989, 'The Regulation of Privatised Monopolies in the UK', *RAND Journal of Economics*, Vol. 20, No. 3.

Bishop, M., Kay, J. and Mayer, C. (eds), 1994, *Privatisation and Economic Performance*, OUP.

Bishop, M. Kay, J. and Mayer, C. (eds) 1995, *The Regulatory Challenge*, OUP.

Borrie, G. 1993, 'How can UK Competition Policy be Improved?' in Beesley, *Major Issues in Regulation*.

Bosanquet, N. 1981, 'Sir Keith's Reading List', Political Quarterly, Vol. 52.

Brauetigam, R. and Panzar, J.C. 1993, 'Effects of the Change from Rate of Return to Price Cap Regulation', *American Economic Review*, May.

Burns, P. (ed.) 1995, *Effective Utility Regulation – The Accounting Requirements*, CRI Proceedings 9.

Burns, P. 1995a, 'How Cost Reflective are Utility Tariffs?' in Burns, *Effective Utility Regulation*.

Burton, J. 1997, 'The Competitive Order or Ordered Competition?', *Public Administration*, Vol. 75, No. 2.

Byatt, I. 1994, Chairman's comments on Mayer, C. 'The Regulation of the Water Industry: an Interim Assessment', in Beesley, *Regulating Utilities: The Way Forward*.

Byatt, I. 1995, 'Water: the Periodic Review Process' in Beesley, *Utility Regulation: Challenge and Response*.

Byatt, I. 1996, Chairman's comments on Glaister, S. 'Incentives in Natural Monopoly: the Case of Water' in Beesley (ed.), 1996.

Byatt, I. 1998, 'Valuing Improvements,' *Utilities Journal*, January.

Campbell, J. 1993, *Edward Heath*, Jonathan Cape.

Carsberg, B. 1994, 'Regulators' Information Requirements' in Burns, *Effective Utility Regulation*.

Carter, N. and Lowe, P. 1995, 'Setting up a Cross-Sector Environment Agency' in Gray, *UK Environmental Policy in the 1990s*.

Cave, M. 1993, 'An Economist's Perspective on Regulating Quality Standards and Levels of Service', in Hicks, *Utilities and Their Customers, Whose Quality of Service is it?*

Chapman, C. 1990, *Selling the Family Silver*, Hutchinson.

Chesshire, J. 1996, 'Energy Efficiency: Some Policy Priorities' in MacKerron and Pearson, *The UK Energy Experience: a Model or a Warning?*

Coen, D. and Willman, P. 1998, 'The Evolution of the Firm's Regulatory Affairs Office', *Business Strategy Review*, Vol. 9, No. 4.

Consumers Association, 1997, *Utilities in Transition – a Consumer Perspective*.

Copley, S. 1994, 'Cost Allocation Methodology in Practice', in Burns, *Effective Utility Regulation*.

Corry, D., Hewett, C. and Tindale, S. (eds) 1996, *Energy '98: Competing for Power*, IPPR.

Cowan, S. 1997, 'Competition in the Water Industry', *Oxford Review of Economic Policy*, Vol. 13, No. 1.

Craig, P. 1987, 'The Monopolies and Mergers Commission: Competition and Administrative Rationality', in Baldwin and McCrudden, *Regulation and Public Law*.

Currie, D. 1997, 'The Labour View' in Beesley, *Regulating the Utilities: Broadening the Debate*.

Department of Trade and Industry, 1993, *The Prospects for Coal*, Cm 2235.

Doble, M. 1999, 'Low Income Consumers in the Competitive Gas Market: Why Don't Pre-payment Meter Users Switch to Cheaper Payment Methods?' *Benefits: a Journal of Social Security Research, Policy and Practice*.

DTI, 1995, *Energy Report*.

DTI, 1998a, *A Fair Deal for Consumers*, Cm 3898.

DTI, 1998b, *Conclusions of the Review of Energy Sources for Power Generation*, Cm. 4071.

DTI, 1999, *Energy Report*.

Edwards, M. 1999, 'Power station Coal in England and Wales: a Circular Process?' *Utilities Journal*, September.

Employment Committee, Session 1992–93, 2nd Report, *Employment Consequences of BC's Proposed Pit Closures*, HC 263.

Employment Committee, Session 1994–95, 3rd Report, *Remuneration of Directors and Chief Executives of Privatised Utilities*, HC 159.

Energy Committee Session 1991–92, 5th Report, *Clean Coal Technology and the Coal Market after 1993*, HC 208.

Energy Committee, Session 1991–92, 2nd Report, *Consequences of Electricity Privatisation*, HC 113.

Environment Committee, Session 1993–94, *Energy Efficiency: the Role of Ofgas*, Minutes of Evidence, HC 328.

Environment Committee, Session 1994–95, *Energy Efficiency*, Minutes of Evidence, HC 229.

Environmental Audit Committee, Session 1998–99, 6th Report, *The Greening Government Initiative 1999*, HC 426.

Environmental Audit Committee, Session 1998–99, 7th Report, *Energy Efficiency*, HC 159.

Ernst, J. 1994, *Whose Utility?* Open University Press.

Evans, R. 1993, 'Customer Rights and Company Duties' in Hicks, *Utilities and their Customers*.

Fairburn, J. and Kay, J. (eds), 1989, *Mergers and Merger Policy*, Oxford University Press.

Foreman-Peck, J. and Milward, R. 1995, *Public and Private Ownership of British Industry 1820–1990*, Clarendon Press.

Foster, Christopher, 1992, *Privatisation, Public Ownership and the Regulation of Natural Monopoly*, Blackwell, Oxford.

Gardener, J. 1993, 'Company Communication with Customers' in Vass, *The Water Industry: New Arrangements and Challenges*.

Gas Consumers Council, 1993, *Annual Report 1993*.

Gas Consumers Council, 1997, *Annual Report 1997*.

Gilbert, R. and Kahn, E. (eds), 1996, *International Comparisons of Electricity Regulation*, Cambridge University Press.

Gilland, T. (ed.) 1993, *Regulatory Policy and the Energy Sector*, CRI.

Gilland, T. and Vass, P. (eds) 1993, *Regulatory Review 1993*, CRI.

Gilmour, I. 1993, *Dancing with Dogma*, Simon and Schuster.

Graham, C. 1993, 'Overview' in Hicks, *Utilities and their Customers: Whose Quality of Service is it?*

Graham, C. 1995, *Is There a Crisis in Regulatory Accountability?* CRI.

Graham, C. 1997, 'Regulatory Responses to MMC Decisions' in Vass, *Regulatory Review 1997*.

Gray, T. (ed.) 1995, *UK Environmental Policy in the 1990s*, Macmillan.

Green, R. and McDaniel, T. 1998, 'Competition in Electricity Supply: Will "1998" be Worth It?' *Fiscal Studies*, Vol. 19, No. 3.

Green, R. and Newbery, D. 1997, 'Competition in the Electricity Industry in England and Wales', *Oxford Review of Economic Policy*, Vol. 13, No. 1.

Hall, C., Scott, C. and Hood, C. 2000, *Telecommunications Regulation: Culture, Chaos and Interdependence*, Routledge.

Harris, K. 1999, 'Water Regulation 1997–98', in Vass, *Regulatory Review 1998–99*.

Hawkins, N. 1994, 'City Perspective: Utilities in the UK' in Vass and Gilland, *Regulatory Review 1994*.

Heald, D. 1988, 'The UK: Privatisation and its Political Context', *West European Politics*, Vol. 11, No. 4.

Helm, D. 1993, 'Energy Policy and Market Doctrine', *Political Quarterly*, Vol. 64, No. 4.

Helm, D. 1994a, 'British Utility Regulation: Theory, Practice and Reform', *Oxford Review of Economic Policy*, Vol. 10, No. 3.

Helm, D. 1994b, 'Regulating the Transition to the Competitive Electricity Market' in Beesley, *Regulating Utilities, the Way Forward*.

Helm, D. (ed.) 1995a, *British Utility Regulation: Principles Experience and Reform*, Oxera Press.

Helm, D. 1995b 'Comments' on Byatt, 'Water: The Periodic Review Process' in Beesley (ed.), *Utility Regulation: Challenge and Response*.

Helm, D. (ed.) 1996, *Economic Policy towards the Environment*, Blackwell.

Helm, D. 1998a, 'Environmental Policy – Objectives, Instruments and Institutions', *Oxford Review of Economic Policy*, Vol. 14, No. 4.

Helm, D. 1998b, 'Environmental Expenditures and the Water Periodic Review', *Utilities Journal*, April.

Helm, D. 1998c, 'Labour and Energy Policy', *Utilities Journal*, September.

Helm, D. 1999, 'Regulatory Reform', *Utilities Journal*, November.

Helm, D. and Jenkinson, T. 1997, 'Introducing Competition into Regulated Industries', *Oxford Review of Economic Policy*, Vol. 13, No. 1.

Helm, D. and Yarrow, J. 1988, 'The Regulation of Utilities', *Oxford Review of Economic Policy*, Vol. 4, No. 2.

Hennessy, P. 1990, *Whitehall*, Fontana.

Hennessy, P. 1994, *Never Again*, Jonathan Cape.

Hennessy, P. 1995, *The Hidden Wiring*, Gollancz.

Hicks, C. (ed.) 1993, *Utilities and their Customers: Whose Quality of Service is it?* Proceedings No. 6, CRI.

Hodges, J. 1998 'Climate Change: Consulting on a New UK Programme', *Utilities Journal*, Vol. 1, October.

Howe, M. 1998, 'The MMC and RPI-X' in Beesley, *Regulating Utilities: Understanding the Issues*.

Jackson, P. and Price, C. (eds), 1994, *Privatisation and Regulation*, Longman.

Jenkins, Simon 1996, *Accountable to None: The Tory Nationalisation of Britain*, Penguin.

Jones, P. (ed.) 1995, *Party, Parliament and Personality*, Routledge.

Jones, T. 1993, 'Privatisation and Market Structure in the Gas Industry' in Clarke and Pitelis, *The Political Economy of Privatisation*, Routledge.

Kay, J. 1996, 'The Future of UK Utility Regulation' in Beesley, *Regulating Utilities: A Time for Change?*

Kelf-Cohen, R. 1969, *20 Years of Nationalisation*, Macmillan.

Lapsley, I. and Kilpatrick, K. 1997, *A Question of Trust: Regulators and the Regulatory Regime for Privatised Utilities*, ICAS, Edinburgh.

Lascelles, D. 1995, 'The Electricity Industry 1994–95', in Vass, *Regulatory Review 1995*.

Lawson, N. 1992, *The View from Number 11*, Bantam.

Littlechild, S. 1988, 'Economic Regulation of Privatised Water Authorities and Some Further Reflections', *Oxford Review of Economic Policy*, Vol. 4, No. 2.

Littlechild, S. 1995, 'Competition in Electricity: Retrospect and Prospect', in Beesley, *Utility Regulation: Challenge and Response*.

Littlechild, S. 1996, 'Privatisation, Competition and Regulation in the Scottish Electricity Industry', *Scottish Journal of Political Economy*, Vol. 43, No. 1.

MacKerron, G. and Boira Segarra, I. 1996, 'Regulation' in Surrey, *The British Electricity Experiment*.

MacKerron, G. and P. Pearson (eds), 1995, *The UK Energy Experience: A Model or a Warning?* Imperial College Press.

Manners, G. 1987, 'British Coal and the Privatising of Electricity Supply', *Public Money*, December.

Manners, G. 1995, 'Energy Conservation Policy' in Gray, *UK Environmental Policy in the 1990s*.

Massey, A. 1993, *Managing the Public Sector*, Edward Elgar.

Mayer, C. 1999, 'A Model Review?' *Utilities Journal*, October.

MMC, 1993, *Gas and British Gas plc*, Vol. 3, Cm 2317.

Morris, D. 1998, 'Utility References and the MMC' in Vass, 1998, *Modernizing the Framework*.

National Audit Office, 1996, *The Work of the Directors General of Telecommunications, Gas Supply, Water Services and Electricity Supply*, HC 645, 1995–96.

National Audit Office, 1999, *Giving Customers a Choice – The Introduction of Competition into the Domestic Gas Market*.

Newbery, D. 1993, 'Impact of EC Environmental Policy on British Coal', *Oxford Review of Economic Policy*, Vol. 9, No. 4.

Newbery, D. and Green, R. 1996, 'Regulation, Public Ownership and Privatisation of the English Electricity Industry' in Gilbert and Kahn (eds), *International Comparisons of Electricity Regulation*.

Newbery, D. and Pollitt, M. 1997, 'Restructuring and Privatisation of Britain's CEGB – Was it Worth it?' *Journal of Industrial Economics*, Vol. XLV.

Newman, K. 1986, *The Selling of British Telecom*, Holt, Rinehart and Winston.

Odgers, G. 1995, 'MMC: Talking Shop or Decision Maker?' in Beesley, *Utility Regulation: Challenge and Response*.

Odgers, G. 1998, 'Reform of UK Competition law', *Utilities Journal*, January.

OFFER, 1997, *Annual Report*.

OFFER, 1998, *Report on Customer Services 1997–8*.

Ofgem, 2000, *Social Action Plan*.

OFTEL, 1999, *Universal Telecommunications Services*.

Ofwat, 1996, *Report on Yorkshire Water Services*.

Ofwat, 1997, *Annual Report*.

Ogden, S. 1997, 'Accounting for Organisational Performance: the Construction of the Customer in the Privatised Water Industry', *Accounting, Organisations and Society*, Vol. 22, No. 6.

Ogden, S. and Anderson, F. 1995, 'Representing Customers' Interests: the case of the privatised water industry in England and Wales', *Public Administration*, Vol. 71, Winter.

Parker, M. 1993, 'Coal privatisation, Competition and Integrated Energy Policy – Free or Managed Market?' in Gilland, *Regulatory Policy and the Energy Sector*.

Parker, M. 1995, 'Decline of UK Coal: Economics or Politics?' in MacKerron and Pearson, *The UK Energy Experience: A Model or a Warning?*

Parker, M. 1998, 'A New Energy Policy?', *Utilities Journal*, November.

Parker, M. and Surrey, J. 1993, 'The October 1992 Coal Crisis and Energy Policy', *Political Quarterly*, Vol. 64, No. 4.

Pitt, D. 1994, 'An Essentially Contestable Organisation: BT and the Privatisation Debate' in J.J. Richardson (ed.), *Privatisation and Deregulation in Britain and Canada*.

Price, C. 1994a, 'Economic Regulation of Privatised Monopolies' in Jackson and Price, *Privatisation and Regulation*.

Price, C. 1994b 'Industry Structure and Network Access Charges' in Vass and Gilland, *Regulatory Review 1994*.

Price, C. 1994c, 'Gas Regulation and Competition: Substitutes or Complements?' in Bishop et al., *Privatisation and Economic Performance*.

Prosser, T. 1986, *Nationalised Industries and Public Control*, Blackwell.

Prosser, T. 1997, *Law and the Regulators*, Oxford University Press.

Public Accounts Committee, Session 1996–97, 16th Report, *The Work of the Directors General of Telecommunications, Gas Supply, Water Services and Electricity Supply*, HC 89.

Public Service Committee, Session 1995–96, 2nd Report, *Ministerial Accountability and Responsibility*, HC 313.

Ramsay, I. 1987, 'The Office of Fair Trading: Policing the Consumer Market Place' in Baldwin and McCrudden, *Regulation and Public Law*.

Ranelagh, J. 1992, *Thatcher's People*, Fontana.

Rees, J. 1994, 'Water Services – the Periodic Review and Beyond', in Vass and Gilland, *Regulatory Review 1994*.

Rees, R. 1986, 'Is There an Economic Case for Privatisation?', *Public Money*, March.

Rhodes, R. 1994, 'The Hollowing Out of the State', *Political Quarterly*, Vol. 65, No. 2.

Richardson, J.J. (ed.) 1990, *Privatisation and Deregulation in Britain and Canada*, Dartmouth.

Ridley, N. 1991, *My Style of Government*, Hutchinson.

Robinson, C. 1994, 'Gas' in Beesley (ed.), *Regulating Utilities: The Way Forward*.

Robinson, C. 1996, 'Electricity' in Beesley, *Regulating Utilities: A Time for Change?*

Robinson, C. (ed.) 2000, *Regulating Utilities: New Problems, New Solutions*, Edward Elgar.

Scott, C., Hall, C. and Hood, C. 1997, 'Regulatory Space and Institutional Reform: The Case of Telecommunications' in Vass, *Regulatory Review 1997*.

Sharratt, D. 2000, 'Fuel Direct: Who Benefits?', *Utilities Journal*, April.

Skea, J. 1995, 'Acid Rain: a Business-as-Usual Scenario' in Gray, *UK Environmental Policy in the 1990s*.

Stelzer, I. 1988, 'Britain's Newest Import: America's Regulatory Experience', *Oxford Review of Economic Policy*, Vol. 4, No. 2.

Stern, J. 1994, 'Gas and the MMC Review' in Vass and Gilland, *Regulatory Review 1994*.

Stiglitz, J. 1998, 'Private Uses of Public Interests: Incentives and Institutions', *Journal of Economic Perspectives*, Vol. 12, No. 2.

Stirling, A. 1992, 'Regulating the Electricity Industry by valuing environmental effects: How much is the Emperor wearing?', *Futures*, Vol. 24, No. 10.

Streeter, R. 1999, 'The Environment Agency' in Vass, *Regulatory Review 1998–99*.

Surrey, J. (ed.) 1996, *The British Electricity Experiment*, Earthscan.

Thatcher, M. 1998, 'Institutions, Regulation and Change: New Regulatory Agencies in the British Privatised Utilities' *West European Politics*, Vol. 21, No. 1.

Trade and Industry Committee (TIC) Session 1991–92, First Report, *Takeovers and Mergers*, HC 90.

TIC, Session 1994–95, 11th Report, *Aspects of the Electricity Supply Industry*, HC 481.

TIC, Session 1994–95, 1st Report, *The Domestic Gas Market*, HC 23.

TIC, Session 1994–95, 5th Report, *UK Policy on Monopolies*, HC 249.

TIC, Session 1996–97, 2nd Report, *Liberalisation of the Electricity Market*, HC 279.

TIC, Session 1996–97, First Report, *Energy Regulation*, March 1997, HC 50.

TIC, Session 1997–98, 10th Report, *Developments in the Liberalisation of the Electricity Market*, HC 871.

TIC, Session 1997–98, 2nd Report, *Progress in the Liberalisation of the gas market*, HC 338.

TIC, Session 1997–98, 4th Report, *Coal*, HC 404.

TIC, Session 1997–98, 5th Report, *Energy Policy*, HC 471.

TIC, Session 1998–99, 9th Report, *Impact on Industry of the Climate Change Levy*, HC 678.

TIC, Session 1999–2000, *The Work of Ofgem*, Evidence, HC 193.

Tierney, S. 1996, 'Ofgas and the Energy Efficiency Debate', *Utilities Law Review*, Vol. 7, February.

Vass, P. 1993, 'Water Services: Preparing for 1994', in Vass, *Regulatory Review 1993*.

Vass, P. (ed.) 1994a, *Regulating the Utilities: Accountability and Processes*, CRI.

Vass, P. 1994b, 'Accountability of Regulators' in Vass and Gilland, *Regulatory Review 1994*.

Vass, P. (ed.) 1995a, *The Water Industry 1995: New Arrangements and Challenges*, Proceedings No. 18, CRI.

Vass, P. (ed.) 1995b, *Regulatory Review 1995*, CRI.

Vass, P. (ed.) 1995c, *Regulated Industries 1995*, CRI and IPPR.

Vass, P. 1995d, 'The UK Water Industry' in Vass, *Regulated Industries 1995*.

Vass, P. (ed.) 1996, *Regulatory Review 1996*, CRI.

Vass, P. (ed.) 1997, *Regulatory Review 1997*, CRI.

Vass, P. (ed.) 1998, *Modernising the Framework: The New Agenda for Regulated Industries*, CRI.

Vass, P. (ed.) 1999, *Regulatory Review 1998–9*, CRI.

Vass, P. 1999a, 'Accounting for Regulation' in Vass, *Regulatory Review, 1998–99*.

Vass, P. and Gilland, T. (eds), 1994, *Regulatory Review 1994*, CRI.

Veljanovski, C. 1987, *Selling the State*, Weidenfeld and Nicolson.

Veljanovski, C. 1994, 'The Need for a Regulatory Charter' in Vass, *Regulating the Utilities: Accountability and Processes*.

Veljanovski, C. (ed.) 1991, *Regulators and the Market*, IEA.

Vickers, J. 1997, 'Regulation, Competition and the Structure of Prices', *Oxford Review of Economic Policy*, Vol. 13, No. 1.

Waddams Price, C. 1997a, 'Undue Discrimination and Cross-Subsidies: Price Structures in UK Utilities', *Utilities Law Review*, Vol. 8, September.

Waddams Price, C. 1997b, 'Competition and Regulation in the UK Gas Industry', *Oxford Review of Economic Policy*, Vol. 13, No. 1.

Waddams Price, C. 1998, Response to the Government's consultation paper on Consumer Councils, mimeo.

Waddams Price, C. 2000, 'Gas: Regulating for Social Needs', in Robinson, *Regulating Utilities: New Issues, New Solutions.*

Waddams Price, C. and Biermann, A. 1998, *Fuel Poverty in Britain*, Ofgas.

Waddams Price, C. and Hancock, R. 1998, 'Distributional Effects of liberalising residential utility markets in the UK', *Fiscal Studies*, August.

Walker, D. 1990, 'Enter the Regulators' *Parliamentary Affairs*, Vol. 43, No. 3.

Ward, Graham 1993, 'Reforming the public sector', *Political Quarterly*, Vol. 64, No. 3.

Waterson, M. 1995, 'Developing Utility Regulation in the UK' in Helm, *British Utility Regulation: Principles, Experience and Reform.*

Weeden, R. 1996, 'Water and Sewerage Services 1995–96' in Vass, *Regulatory Review 1996.*

Westlake, B. 1997, 'The Electricity Industry 1996–7', in Vass, *Regulatory Review 1997.*

Weyman-Jones, T. 1995, 'Problems of Yardstick Regulation in Electricity Distribution' in Bishop, Kay and Meyer, 1995.

Wilks, S. 1993, 'The Office of Fair Trading in Administrative Context' in Vass, *Regulating the Utilities: Accountability and Processes.*

Wilks, S. 1997, *Accountability and the Growth of the Regulatory State In Britain*, paper prepared for the XVIIth World Congress of the IPSA, Seoul.

Wolin, S. 1961, *Politics and Vision*, Allen and Unwin.

Wright, V. 1995, 'The Industrial Privatisation Programmes of Britain and France' in Jones (ed.), *Party, Politics and Personality.*

Yarrow, G. 1996, 'Dealing with Social Obligations in Telecoms' in Beesley, *Regulating Utilities: A Time for Change?*

Young, H. 1991, *One of Us*, Macmillan.

Index